THE TECHNIQUE OF CHORAL
COMPOSITION

LONDON : HUMPHREY MILFORD

OXFORD UNIVERSITY PRESS

The Technique of Choral Composition

BY

ARCHIBALD T. DAVISON

James Edward Ditson Professor of Music
Harvard University

CAMBRIDGE, MASSACHUSETTS
HARVARD UNIVERSITY PRESS
1945

To

RANDALL THOMPSON

FIRST AMONG OUR NATIVE COMPOSERS IN THE
ART OF CHORAL WRITING

PREFACE

THE author's purpose in this book has been to furnish the student with such practical information as will enable him efficiently to manipulate choral material without reference to a specific period or style and, furthermore, to avoid burdening him with an excess of technical minutiae. To be sure, examples, admonitions, precepts, and lists of devices associated with the composition of choral music might be multiplied almost without number, but the author would be most unwilling to offer such a detailed manual of procedure for an enterprise which presupposes originality, ingenuity, and imagination. He has selected for inclusion only the material which he believes to be fundamentally important and which, over a long period of years as a teacher of choral technique, he has found most useful to students entering on a study of this branch of the art. The resourceful worker — and he alone should undertake the task — will discover, once he has gained facility, how many corollaries there are to each theorem herein enunciated.

Only incidental historical matter has been included, and no effort has been made to deal chronologically with the development of choral method. Admittedly a study of sixteenth-century choral technique is far more than a beneficent discipline. From it one learns respect for the individuality of the single line, for rhythmic flexibility within that line, and for the inevitable propriety of text distribution. No age whose counterpoint frankly acknowledges the presence of harmony can teach these lessons as convincingly as the Golden Age. But the student should seek in the music of the sixteenth century the basic principles of choral truth rather than models of composition, for even the best imitations of Palestrina are pathetically anachronistic.

The brief musical examples are not always submitted as

models of style, but rather as illustrations of choral device. Some of them are witnesses to the fact that matter may be far inferior to manner, and these are introduced only because they are unequivocal demonstrations of choral aptitude. Any musical excerpt loses its significance if it is treated as an isolated case, and its full meaning is apparent only in the light of the context which surrounds it. The student is urged, therefore, to build up a choral library of his own containing as many as possible of the pieces represented by the illustrations accompanying the text, and by the supplementary examples offered in the appendix. This advice would be unreasonable had the author proceeded with the idea of presenting something like a catalogue of choral music in various styles. He has, indeed, done just the reverse. He has included only the most characteristic illustrations, and he has drawn as many as possible from a single source. Availability has generally, though not invariably, dictated the selection of the editions from which the illustrations have been drawn.

A two-staff score has been used wherever possible, and unless another medium is indicated, the reader may assume the illustration to be for mixed voices. Accompaniments have been omitted except where they bear a definite relation to the matter in hand. In many cases the texting is fragmentary, offering only enough words to furnish some idea of the meaning of the passage. Furthermore, indications such as dynamic marks and slurs have generally been left out. Most of these economies are necessary in order to make the music easily readable, as well as to conserve space; and they emphasize the need for an examination of the whole score.

Every composition, whether merely referred to in the text of the book, or represented by a musical excerpt, is listed in the index of compositions together with the publisher and the edition used. There are also lists of publishers and of choral collections with their abbreviations.

For the author to express his gratitude to those who assisted him in the preparation of this book may seem to be no more than the customary gesture. It is, indeed, far more than that. The music illustrations, by all means the most important part of this book, were copied by Mr. John Scabia, whose precise and artistic workmanship bears witness to an interest that was more than professional. My colleague, Professor G. Wallace Woodworth, read the text with critical care, and aided me immeasurably by his suggestions. Regarding numerous matters I sought the advice of Professor Donald J. Grout of the University of Texas whose wise and untiring counsel never failed to resolve my perplexities. And last, I offer my heartfelt thanks to my wife, by whose generous and artful dissembling the painstaking care of manifold and wearisome detail was made to seem the lightest of diversions.

Finally, it may be said that in one mechanical aspect, at least, the task of writing this book would have been materially lightened had some daring inventor of words come to grips with the problem of substituting a single noun for the many circumlocutions employed as descriptive of the process of setting music to text. Any author may justifiably deplore the necessity imposed upon him by the inflexibility of a language that sends him forth on his literary journey with such cumbersome linguistic luggage as "writing for voices," "choral method," "vocal scoring" and "the technique of choral composition." These, and similar phrases, must be dragged from page to page in endless variation. The reader is doubtless already weary of them. Essentially they all mean the same thing, and the one word "chorestration" would prove an effective substitute for them all. Fearful of being suspected of possessing a penchant for logomachy, the author contents himself with the hope that this little seed of suggestion or another yet more fruitful will sometime take root within the covers of the dictionary.

A. T. D.

CAMBRIDGE
May, 1944

ACKNOWLEDGMENTS

THE AUTHOR gratefully acknowledges the kindness of the publishers or their American representatives who have given permission to reproduce from copyrighted works the examples of choral music in this book. The companies and the works from which excerpts are drawn are as follows:

To Associated Music Publishers, Inc., New York, for Hindemith's "The Harp That Once Thro' Tara's Halls"; to the same company, copyright owners, for Schönberg's "Six Pieces for Male Chorus," Thomas' "Passionsmusik (Markus)," Hindemith's "Neues vom Tage," "Bastellied," and "Das Unaufhörliche," Janáček's "Festliche Messe," Křenek's "Die Jahreszeiten," Milhaud's "Psaume 121," and Szymanowski's "Stabat Mater."

To Augener Ltd., London, for Schubert's "Mass in B flat Major."

To C. C. Birchard & Co., Boston, for Malipiero's "La Cena" and "The Princess Ulalia," and Roussel's "Psalm 80."

To Boosey & Hawkes, Inc., New York, copyright owners, for Kodály's "Psalmus Hungaricus" and "Evening," and Delius' "Requiem."

To The Boston Music Co., Boston, for Reger's "Evening Song."

To J. & W. Chester Ltd., London, for Malipiero's "San Francesco d'Assisi," and Stravinsky's "Les Noces."

To J. Curwen & Sons, London (for the U.S.A. G. Schirmer, Inc., New York), for Holst's "A Dirge for Two Veterans" and "I Love My Love," G. Williams' "Richard of Taunton Dene," and Vaughan Williams' "Sancta Civitas" and "The Turtle Dove."

To H. F. W. Deane & Sons, London (C. C. Birchard & Co., Boston, American agents), for Parry's "There Is an Old Belief."

To Oliver Ditson Co., Philadelphia, for Bantock's "Lady of the Lagoon," Mendelssohn's "Loreley," Rossini's "Messe Solonnelle," Saint-Saëns' "Noel," and Tschaikowsky's "The Nightingale."

To Durand & Cie, Paris, France, and Elkan-Vogel Co., Inc., Philadelphia, for Caplet's "Inscriptions Champêtres," "Trois Chants d'Église," and "Le Miroir de Jésus," Debussy's "Trois Chansons," Ravel's "Trois Chansons," Roussel's "Padmâvatî," and Saint-Saëns' "La Nuit."

To Édition Russe de Musique, Paris (Galaxy Music Corporation, New York), for Stravinsky's "Symphonie de Psaumes."

To J. Fischer & Bro., New York, for Tschelishcheff's "Cherubim Song."

To Foetisch Frères (S.A.), Lausanne, Switzerland, for Honegger's "King David."

To The H. W. Gray Co., Inc., New York, for Holst's "Funeral Hymn."

To The Frederick Harris Music Co. Ltd., Oakville, Ontario, for Willan's "An Apostrophe to the Heavenly Host."

To Novello and Co. Ltd., London (agents, The H. W. Gray Co., Inc., New York), for Bach's "The Passion According to St. Matthew," Beethoven's "Mount of Olives," Bliss's "Pastoral" and "Morning Heroes," Elgar's "Psalm 48," Gluck's "Orpheus," Gounod's "Mors et Vita," Graun's "Te Deum," Handel's "Jubilate" and "L'Allegro," Haydn's "Mass in C major" and "The Creation," Holst's "First Choral Symphony," Liszt's "St. Elizabeth," Mendelssohn's "St. Paul," "Elijah," and "Lauda Sion," Mozart's "Requiem Mass," Purcell's "O Sing unto the Lord" and "King Arthur," Rossini's "Stabat Mater," Schumann's "Manfred," and Weber's "Mass in E flat major."

To Oxford University Press, London, and Carl Fischer, Inc., New York, American agents, for Lambert's "The Rio Grande," Tallis' "Audivi Vocem de Coelo," and "Lamentations," Walton's "Belshazzar's Feast," Vaughan Williams' "Benedicite" and "Shepherds of the Delectable Mountains."

To C. F. Peters, Leipzig (Clayton F. Summy Co., Chicago, American agents), for Astorga's "Stabat Mater," Bach's "Magnificat," Beethoven's "Mass in C major," Brahms's "Ach lieber Herre Jesu Christ," Cherubini's "Requiem in C minor," Durante's "Magnificat," Monteverdi's "Piagn'e sospira," Mozart's "Vesperae de Dominica," and Schumann's "Requiem für Mignon."

To G. Ricordi & Co. Inc., New York, for Gastoldi's "Al Mormorar," Gesualdo's "Donna se m'ancidete," and Pizzetti's "Requiem Mass."

To Rouart, Lerolle & Cie, Paris, France, and Elkan-Vogel Co. Inc., Philadelphia, for Pierné's "Les Cathédrales."

To E. C. Schirmer Music Co., Boston, for Brahms's "Schicksalslied," Ford's "Since First I Saw Your Face," Mendelssohn's "Der Jäger Abschied," Paxton's "How sweet, how fresh," R. Thompson's "Alleluia," "The Peaceable Kingdom," and "Quis multis gracilis."

To G. Schirmer, Inc., New York, for Bach's "Ode of Mourning" and "God's Time Is the Best," Berlioz' "The Damnation of Faust" and "Requiem," Beethoven's "Ninth Symphony" (choral finale), Brahms's "Requiem," Cui's "The Two Roses," Dubois's "Paradise Lost," Dvorák's "Stabat Mater," Fauré's "Madrigal" and "The Birth of Venus," Franck's "The Beatitudes," G. Gabrieli's "Beata es Virgo Maria" and "Jubilate Deo," Gretchaninoff's "Sun and Moon," Handel's "Messiah," Haydn's "Mass in D minor" and "The Seasons," Hofhaimer's "Herzliebstes Bild," Liszt's "Missa Solennis," Palestrina's "Stabat Mater," Schumann's "Gypsy Life," Schütz's "Song of Praise," Sweelinck's "O Seigneur, loué sera," Taneyeff's "Sunrise," Verdi's "Requiem," Wagner's "Die Meistersinger," and Weber's "Mass in G major."

To Stainer & Bell, Ltd., London (Galaxy Music Corporation, New York), for Byrd's "Praise our Lord all ye Gentiles," Holst's "Autumn Song" and "The Hymn of Jesus," and Vaughan Williams' "A Sea Symphony."

CONTENTS

THE TECHNIQUE OF CHORAL
COMPOSITION

INTRODUCTION

THERE will probably always be debate as to whether vocal music, even the best of it, is worthy to take rank with the products of instrumental genius — whether Schubert's songs and Bach's *B minor Mass,* measured by the arbitrary yardstick of aesthetic theory, are really the equal of Beethoven's "Emperor" concerto and Mozart's "Jupiter" symphony. These questions are, at most, of academic interest, for the irrefutable fact is that Schubert's songs and the *B minor Mass* are immortal. Vocal music needs no apology, and though the speculative aesthetician may find reason to disparage it, it has at least some reasons for being to which instrumental music may not lay claim. The musical instrument is, in essence, a machine, and in the hands of many a performer its mechanical status is, alas, all too apparent. Whoever for the first time holds in his hand a clarinet with its bewildering array of keys, or seats himself before a modern organ, must feel strongly that he faces something which is first of all a highly complex machine and after that, perhaps, a musical instrument. No art is more intensely *human* and less mechanical than music; surely there is nothing in this universe that is more *alive.* But with every mechanical device that we interpose between the initial heat of creative imagination and the transference of that heat into interpretative effort, the distance between us and the composer grows greater. This is, indeed, one advantage which vocal music possesses over instrumental — that a supremely human message is transmitted by the most direct human means with which we are endowed. Never, except in the hands of a performer to whom the mechanics of his instrument are as the mechanics of breathing, is the rôle of a really eloquent interpreter confided; whereas in the case of the chorus in particular, it is the *absence* of purely mechanical perfection and the *presence* of those human and unpredictable elements, that help to make performance stimulating and convincing.

In this distinction there is no implied hostility or even rivalry between voices and instruments; each fills its place as only it can in the total scheme of music; each has its own peculiar properties which composers rely on to render their ideas alive. In the end, it is not the medium in which a work is cast that will dictate our judgment concerning the greatness of a specific composition, but, rather, the extent to which it proclaims the inspiration of its maker and the technical skill with which it is set forth.

Categories of music based on an estimate of the relative value of whole fields of musical art, and opinions as to what makes one work greater than another, are not, after all, the primary concern of the student of composition. They relate to the music and not to its creator. For the beginner there is a far more important matter; one by no means remote from those which have just been dealt with; and recognition of its significance and an understanding of its implications may, in the end, determine the direction the student's work will take.

This profoundly interesting matter — and it is one not overmuch pursued — concerns the susceptibility of composers to the varying types of stimulus which lead to creative activity. In other words just how and why does a particular composer's imagination work? Lowes in his monumental study *The Road to Xanadu* [1] has analyzed in detail the imaginative processes of the poet Coleridge and has even ferreted out the substantial details which initiated those processes. In the field of music, however, the problem is much more delicate, for one is dealing in great part with mystery. Schweitzer [2] has attempted to read the mind of Bach, and Rolland [3] has done something of the sort for Beethoven, but, on the whole, the subject remains un-

---

[1] John L. Lowes, *The Road to Xanadu* (Boston: Houghton Mifflin Co., 1930).
[2] Albert Schweitzer, *J. S. Bach*, 2 vols. (London: A. and C. Black, Ltd., 1923).
[3] Romain Rolland, *Beethoven The Creator* (New York: Harper and Bros., 1929).

explored. It is, of course, a vast problem, and capable of a multitude of ramifications. What is creative musical imagination? How does it differ from that of the writer or painter? Why should it react to varying types of ideas? Can anyone explain why Schubert could write one work after another as fast as he was able to procure manuscript paper, drawing only from the wellspring of his musical feeling unprompted by any external suggestion, while Liszt was forever reaching out for the story, the poem or the picture as a subject for his music? Was it something more than aesthetic conviction, an imaginative deficiency, perhaps, or just a type of imagination different from Schubert's, that made Liszt a specialist in the field of program music? In short, can the cold, factual substance of borrowed ideas, regardless of how much it may be touched by eloquence, ever stir emotion or project invention as native fancy may do?

Why do certain imaginations respond almost exclusively to a single medium? Chopin thought in terms of the pianoforte, Wagner in those of the music-drama. Why, in fact, do not *all* composers react to *all* types of music? Is it not extraordinary that in an age ridden by opera Bach could not extend his manifold genius to encompass a single work in this form? There has never been a composer with a more versatile technique than Brahms, yet he too withheld his hand from operatic composition. Why, in the case of a single musician, should the flame of inspiration burn high in one field and appreciably diminish in another? Neither Byrd nor Palestrina, as secular composers, ever approached the heights they achieved as writers of sacred music. Handel, whose suites often sound routine, was, in choral matters, a veritable Titan. Even the Beethoven of the last quartets could sometimes, in his choral music, descend to ideas that are little more than commonplace.

It is easy, of course, to say that for better or worse a composer will not write in a medium that does not attract him. Morales, the sixteenth-century Spanish musician, deliberately refrained from the composition of secular music because he believed that writing in that field constituted a misuse of God's gift to him of the power to create. Musicians do not, however, generally inform us so precisely just why they find one type of composition appealing and another not. Take the case of Sibelius. In view of his great success as a symphonist and the preponderance of his orchestral music, it is difficult to believe that he is exceedingly enamored of the chorus. Why, then, does he trouble to invade a field of expression that reveals him as less than himself? One may explain a lapse in musical quality by the fact that a composer produced certain works simply because it was part of his job to do so. This, of course, does not apply to Sibelius, but in view of Mozart's transcendent genius one can think of no better excuse for most of his masses. Or, where a single field of composition is concerned, one may ascribe ineptness or a paucity of ideas to some technical deficiency. This, indeed, would seem to be one explanation of Schubert's choral music, for Schubert was no contrapuntist, and without counterpoint choral composition is seldom rewarding. However, any thought that the imposition of ready-made ideas as represented by a text set any limits on the power of Schubert's musical expression is immediately dispelled by a recollection of his immortal songs. But does it really answer the question to charge off Mozart's church music to compulsion, the absence of any operatic essay by Brahms to indifference, or Schubert's choral incapacity to a technical limitation? At some time almost every composer must have considered undertaking an opera; and many, having selected a good libretto, have waited for the pot of imagination to boil. For some it has and for others it has not, and the composers themselves would, of all people, probably be the least competent to explain their own success or failure. Will it do merely to say that they were or were not gifted in that quarter? Is there not some salient psychological factor which ought, perhaps, to be taken into account?

To a composer whose imagination runs freest when it is shackled by no objective details such as the presence of words, vocal composition offers inescapable difficulties. One feels, for example, that in many cases, although the text appealed strongly to the composer, imagination was circumscribed by the necessity of building up the music into a line-by-line, almost word-by-word, setting. Morley deals frankly with the matter when he says of the composition of the fantasie, "In this may more art be showne than in any other musicke, because the composer is tied to nothing but that he may adde, diminish, and alter at his pleasure." [4] And Michael Praetorius, dealing with the same issue, says, "A capriccio or extemporized Fantasia results when one sets about elaborating a Fuga [i.e. a fugal theme] according to his own pleasure and fancy, yet does not linger on it for long but soon lights on another Fuga which may come into his mind. For just as in a regular Fuga [i.e. a fugal Ricercare] no text may be underlaid, so here also one is not bound to words, [and] may make much or little, may digress, add, subtract, turn and twist as he will." [5] A third mention of this dilemma is made by Christopher Simpson in connection with his remarks on Fancies for viols, "In this sort of Musick the Composer (being not limited to words) doth imploy all his Art and Invention solely about the bringing in and carrying on of these Fuges, according to the Order and Method formerly shewed." [6] But if a text is sometimes a mill-stone around the composer's neck because it fetters the work-ings of his imagination, remember, too, that words may also serve as a beneficent check on certain types of expression. If you have a perfervid imagination that runs to formlessness or to disregard of reasonable length, you may write either in-cohate or endless instrumental music. Delius is a fair example of the first, Bruckner a first-class example of the second. A text is bound to deal with a limited number of ideas calling for musical treatment, and when you have exhausted these you

[4] Thomas Morley, *A Plaine and Easie Introduction to Practicall Musicke* [Im-printed at London by Humfrey Lownes, dwelling on Bredstreet hill at the signe of the Star], 1608, p. 181.

[5] M. Praetorius, *Syntagma Musicum* (Wolfenbüttel, 1619; ed. E. Bernouilli, Leip-zig: C. F. Kahnt Nachf., 1916), III, 33. (The passage quoted in the text is translated by Lloyd Hibberd.)

[6] Christopher Simpson, *A Compendium of Practical Musick* (London: Printed by William Godbid for Henry Brome in Little Britain, 1667), pp. 141, 142.

are done. Hence, Delius' choral music represents his most trenchant utterance and Bruckner's *Te Deum*, by reason of its brevity in comparison with his other works, makes the heart rejoice. Wagner is an interesting case. While even his most devoted admirers never claimed that a more ample exposition of the substance would enhance the distinction of his music, his detractors have viewed the imposing length of his works as among his lesser aesthetic sins. The theory that when a composer is done with his text the matter is finished will not hold in Wagner's case, because he wrote his own libretti and could make them of any length he chose. His genius was essentially programistic. So, of course, was Liszt's; but the latter's programism was at its best only when it was confined to the instrumental medium, whereas Wagner's programism was invariably underlaid by words either sung or unsung. Critics have insisted that Wagner's imagination responded most actively in the direction of instrumental music and that the vocal sections of his later works are mechanically superimposed on the orchestral texture. But there is much to be said for the opposite view. Those extended instrumental commentaries are not, in reality, interludes; they are narratives; for there is always an implied text concealed within them; words to which no voice, certainly, is given, but which serve as connectives between those parts of the drama which actually are sung. It is not difficult, even, to hear a vocal part running through the Siegfried Idyl. Is it this mysterious element, this imaginary song, that gives continuity to music which, if considered purely instrumental, might be open to the charge of being somewhat long-winded and diffuse? In any case, Wagner seems to present the phenomenon of a composer whose imagination drew from a common source both for instrumental and for vocal music, namely, the wellspring of language.

Composers in any age, unless, like Wagner, they write their own texts, are dealing with ideas which came to them at second hand; the music, unlike the text, must be the composer's own; but it must also be so spontaneous and so at one with the spirit of the words that it will seem, together with those words, to be the work of a single creator. There must be no halting invention; identity of meaning between the music and every item of the text must be continuous and uncalculated. This, by itself, may well give the composer pause. But it constitutes only a part of his difficulty. A less theoretical problem is presented by the requirement of a rhythmic flow which shall, as nearly as possible, match the inflections of the text. It is the age-old problem of escaping the inflexible stress imposed upon music by the metrical provisions of poetry and the dance. It was in the sixteenth century that dissatisfaction with textual conditions reached its peak, and composers of surprisingly different tastes and endowments applied themselves to the issue. Not a few found a solution in the adoption of *vers mesuré* which frankly abandoned regular metre in favor of the classical foot. That, however, was a brief, albeit a fascinating, adventure, and the rhythmic dilemma is as active today as it ever was. Ability to accompany verbally expressed ideas with music of at least equal eloquence, and skill in overcoming the intractable tyrannies of metre — these are problems intrinsic in the composition of both songs and choruses; and all questions of originality and technical equipment aside, the student, if he cannot solve them successfully, should direct his creative energies into other channels.

Song writing has been called an art in miniature; but that remark surely cannot be held true of choral writing. There a single canvas may be as spacious as would be required for three symphonies, and even in the shorter forms, particularly in *a cappella* style, the opportunities for the display of artistic insight, of the refinements of a special skill, and of a power to characterize human emotion are unlimited. It might be supposed, indeed, that a concentrated study of the technique of writing for combined voices would be viewed by most creative musicians as an important factor in their equipment. Yet it is evident to anyone whose work has been extensively connected with choral music that amazingly few composers, even among the great, have passed a reasonable apprenticeship in the handling of choral material. There is, of course, no lack of effective literature. Any competent workman will see to it that his music can be made to *sound*. But from the close of the sixteenth century on, one discovers composer after composer who apparently had more than a casual interest in choral writing; their works often embody ideas of great beauty; the choral dress that clothes them, however, is routine and sometimes even inept. Composers of our own time have profited little from the example of the past, for much of their output is no more than choral hack work, and the achievement of those whose gifts are outstanding shines with a lustre that is sometimes exaggerated by the feeble craftsmanship of the great majority of their colleagues.

Exactly the reverse is true of the orchestral field. While a few composers have been counted as deficient in their handling of the orchestra, skill in instrumentation has generally been taken for granted, and the number of able orchestrators is legion. This is not to say that individuality, inventiveness or genius in instrumentation as one finds these in Berlioz, Wagner, Rimsky-Korsakoff, Holst, and Ravel are musical commonplaces; but one may fairly make the observation that among orchestrators there are many more who approach these men in brilliance than there are choral writers who are rivals of Handel, Mendelssohn, and Brahms.

These three composers, in particular, might be called "choral-minded." They were not only trained in the art of writing for voices and possessed of experience in choral ways; they had, besides, a kind of sixth sense which amounted to choral infallibility. Exactly to describe that instinct would be difficult. It was, perhaps, an unerring feeling for what is vocally profitable. In key selection, in grouping, in the total setting, and in the treatment of the individual parts there was a *rightness* that left nothing to be desired. With the singers they went the second mile. It would even seem that they must have sung each part that they wrote, so natural and effortless is it for the performer. The "choral-minded" composers who flourished after the Golden Age could easily be counted on the fingers of both hands; and for the student who is aiming at choral competence and more, no better counsel could be offered than to study with analytical thoroughness the works of these men, particularly the three mentioned above.[7]

Earlier in these pages the question was raised as to why Sibelius, whose choral output is generally undistinguished, should have taken the trouble to write for voices. Sibelius alone, of course, could resolve that speculation. But many lesser composers are undoubtedly drawn to the chorus because they have a far better chance of gaining a performance than have those who write for the orchestra, albeit to be known as a symphonist is the ambition of probably 90 per cent of the musicians who commit their ideas to music paper. They look askance at the suggestion that a grasp of the refinements of choral technique presupposes much more than a review of the work of those who are recognized as masters in this field, and they assume that compared with the complex resources of the modern orchestra, the limited physique of the chorus makes it unnecessary for one possessing the staple details of the composer's technique to know much more about voices than the limits of their range.

There is, however, a choral technique as expert and as subtle as that for the orchestra, and the management of it in its more

[7] In drawing his conclusions from a study of choral works, the student is urged to put a minimum of trust in the pianoforte. Although the most readily available means, it is most unsatisfactory as an interpreter of vocal music. Aside from hearing an actual performance of the music, the most reliable approach is through the eye, which will respond in proportion to its owner's choral experience both as performer and listener. This counsel is no less valid where the writing of choral music is concerned.

The critic is justly suspicious of choral music that plays too facilely, and there is an abundance of literature for singers that proclaims its pianistic origin. One may take as an example the imitative section in Schumann's *Gypsy Life* to the words

"About the bright fire on their cushion of green,
The men, wild and fearless, reclining are seen."

This passage is far more effective when played than when sung. The student is urged, therefore, to use the piano only for the purpose of trueing-up his work and under no circumstances to allow his fingers to dictate the motion of the voices. To *think* vocally should be the choral composer's habit.

skilful manifestations demands even greater ingenuity than is required in instrumentation. How true this is will appear from a comparative survey of choral with orchestral resource. Let us take only three details — range, dynamic, and color. The choral composer must limit himself to a range of four and one half octaves; the orchestrator may command far more than that. The dynamic potentialities of instruments include an infinity of gradations from the whispering of the strings to the overwhelming volume of the full orchestra. The choral composer must know that he may expect no more by way of pianissimo than a capricious vocal mechanism will permit, and that, at the other extreme, if singers are allowed to give their all, the result may be no more than uncontrolled noise. The timbre of the flute has nothing in common with that of the trombone; nor the quality of the violin with that of the horn. But all voices are generically uniform. The bass is lower than the soprano, it is true, but these, with the alto and tenor, are fundamentally members of a single "consort." The interlacing of parts, the deft manipulation of special areas of the range, and the sudden contrasting of the higher voices with the lower will yield some color variety; even so, these comparatively slight offsets to monotony are to a great extent negatived when the composer is dealing separately with men's voices or with women's voices. Furthermore, except in the case of the national music of certain countries where pulsatile effects are germane, all efforts to transfer from the orchestra to the chorus the particular contribution made by instruments of percussion are bound to lead the composer into artificiality. The chorus may never drive its ship against a rock with such a convincing suggestion of catastrophe as is found in *Scheherazade*. Nor may it arouse the same degree or kind of excitement in the hearer that awakes with those soft insinuating thumps of the bass drum in Berlioz' Hungarian March from the *Damnation of Faust*.

From all this it is clear that the choral composer must to the best of his ability make virtues of his limitations; he must ferret out every legitimate artistic means of impressiveness; and one road to the acquisition of this is certainly, as has been suggested, a careful analysis of the method of those who are eminent as choral writers. Such study, however, is most valuable when it serves as a reinforcement of knowledge gained in three ways: by a study of the technical branches of composition, by the application to those branches of a method that is idiomatically choral, and last, but by no means of least importance, by experience.

It may be assumed that the student will undergo a systematic training in harmony; but without a thorough, and one might say, almost an intuitive command of every resource of counterpoint, he should never enter the field of choral composition. One need but recall the vast and sterile bulk of harmonically conceived choruses, not a few of them the products of the romantic era, prodded into a semblance of artistic vitality by every device of rhythmic ingenuity, yet possessing little power to sustain interest. It would be unreasonable to deny the validity of harmony in contrast to counterpoint as a choral medium. Even before there had set in the strong reaction against counterpoint which characterized the age succeeding that of Bach, choral composers had made the salutary discovery of the value of alternating harmony and counterpoint; but once the dominance of harmony over musical thinking was established, choral music became an artistic stepchild, and beyond that status it has rarely advanced even to our own time.

Except as it bears on the quality of his musicianship, the study of musical forms is not essential to the training of a choral composer. The one form of which he should have detailed knowledge is the fugue. Not only should he understand its structure, but he should be able to compose it. The fugue *in extenso* is normally found only in choral works of some length; and these works are almost without exception accompanied by the orchestra. It goes without saying, then, that the choral composer who wishes to equip himself thoroughly will not neglect the study of instrumentation, especially as it applies to vocal accompaniment. Unskilful orchestration may ruin a vocal effect; there are, however, principles of scoring which not only allow voices full scope for their powers, but which also enhance the beauty of the music by instrumental coloring and in a varied multitude of ways.

The transference of all the foregoing into terms of effectiveness involves the student in practice carried on under supervision. But that instruction will be most valuable if it is supplemented by putting his music to the test of performance. In this detail the student of choral writing is more happily endowed than one working in the field of instrumentation. Few indeed are the opportunities for the budding orchestrator to submit his work to proof. For one who is ambitious to attain skill in choral composition, however, the formation of a small group of amateur singers who will charitably volunteer their services for his benefit is not an insurmountable project. Furthermore, unlike the rare "try-overs" of the work of the incipient orchestral composer which, for him, are often little more than occasions when his piece is two or three times "passed in review" before him, the rehearsals of choral pieces may be of actual laboratory calibre, in that not only the total effect may be carefully assayed through repeated hearings, but also even short sections and single measures may be sung again and again.

The studies which have been described furnish the technique necessary for the practice of the art of choral writing. They connect themselves mainly with textbooks, scores, and courses of study. They are, indeed, indispensable, but their value is doubled by the kind of learning that alone derives from experience won by active participation. All who pursue intensively the study of choral style should, if possible, conduct a chorus, should at least sing regularly in one, and should attend rehearsals of choral organizations of which they are not members. From actual conducting one acquires to an extent which is otherwise impossible an idea of the inner workings of amateur vocal psychology; he discovers what, beyond the implications of the printed page, the composer may expect from the singer. He becomes familiar with vocal capacities and limitations both of physique and of musicianship; where, for example, within the advisable extremes of range, the chorus is at its best. Little by little he will even begin to identify certain notes in each voice as peculiarly effective; and perhaps the most valuable lesson that he will learn from such observation is that it is the text which, before all else, governs the composer's method. For example, the note *F* above middle *C* in the choral tenor voice is one of peculiar beauty from the point of view of quality. Although its timbre will depend to some extent upon the proportion of first and second tenors in the section, its character will be determined mainly by the idea which the composer wishes to convey, an idea which is resident in the text. Thus the word "love" sung at this pitch by the tenors may seem, because of the tone possibilities of the vowel, to suggest all that the word implies; the identical pitch used for the word "hate" may, for the same reason, be used to typify the very embodiment of ill will.

Singing in a chorus, as well as conducting one, has great potential value for the student of choral style, for it permits him to enter acutely into every vocal problem. And in this particular the student of choral music again has a great advantage. Not many of those engaged in learning instrumentation are equipped for orchestral playing; almost everyone, however, has enough vocal endowment to warrant his participation in chorus singing. Whatever the *quality* of his work may eventually prove to be, he will be bound, as a composer, to deal more understandingly with the frailties which, in many guises, afflict the choralist. As a further resource, the following of scores during rehearsals in which the student is not participating will enable him to receive immediate aural confirmation of technical expertness on the one hand, or, on the other, of awkwardness in manipulation of the material.

In the end it will come to him, and perhaps not too reas-suringly, that in the long run the choral composer is more at the mercy of the agencies which bring his work to perform-ance than is his orchestral brother. The latter may count on it that in most cases his score will be confided to players of professional rank; the former must put his trust in the amateur chorus, at best a fallible instrument. The symphonist may feel, of course, that the treatment accorded his composition pain-fully distorts the ideas which the work contains; but as these are not, except in the case of program music, and then, only to a modified extent, susceptible of a common understanding, the hearer is free to submit the composer's meaning to the action of his own imagination. A skilled conductor will sometimes follow his own interpretation of the composer's ideas and pro-duce results even more eloquent than the composer himself envisioned. Quite different is the situation when choral music is in question. There the composer is dealing with ready-made ideas expressed in words which, it may be assumed, are uni-versally apprehensible; and the poetic content of these he seeks to enhance by his music. The conductor, acting on behalf of the composer, is first of all enjoined to make every detail of that text crystal clear; otherwise the music, from the hearer's standpoint, has no reason for being. Beyond this, the composer will fare according to the imagination and resourcefulness of the director. It is he who must consider questions of tempo, dynamics, phrasing, the coloring of vowels to suit the meaning of a particular word, and, in general, the necessity of eliciting from the chorus every last emotional implication of the text, and of imparting to the performance a sense that there are not two elements involved, text and music; not two ideas, the one expressed in notes, the other in words; but, rather, a single artistic unit conveying a single poetic idea.

If the discipline which has been set forth seems unduly ardu-ous, implying something idealistic rather than practical, it should be pointed out that more than one composer has missed total greatness only because he was deficient in choral craftsmanship. Admittedly the way is not short, nor is it easy; and he who pursues it with patience and persistence to the end may, after all, win no more than a conscientious workman's reward; for the success of his music will, in the end, be judged by the power of his eloquence and by his gifts as a creative artist.

CHAPTER I

CHORAL CLEFS, RANGE, AND GROUPING

THE CLEFS generally employed in choral writing are identical with those used in pianoforte music; the *G* clef for the Soprano, Alto, and Tenor, and the *F* clef for the Bass. As the tenor sings an octave lower than the pitch indicated by the notes in his part, the plain *G* clef is not an accurate usage, and signs like 🎼 *or* 🎼 *or, rarely* 🎼 are sometimes found; nonetheless it is common practice to write the simple *G* clef at the beginning of the tenor part, and that custom, therefore, will be followed throughout this book.

The bulk of chorus singing is carried on under nonprofessional auspices, and the composer of choral music may assume that his work will, in a great majority of cases, be performed by a group of amateurs. This fact in no sense conditions his method as it does that of the composer in instrumental forms, because the corporate ability of the amateur chorus will generally match those particular virtues which we commonly ascribe to the professional singer as an individual. In the vocal mechanism with which nature has endowed humanity, she has made no distinction between the trained and the untrained singer, and it is with the physical properties of voices that the composer is first concerned; with the quality of each part in its various ranges; with its normal compass; and beyond that how high or how low it is advisable or even safe to write; and how long the chorus may be counted on to sustain extremes of range, particularly at the top, without discomfort to the singers and without incurring the danger of flatting.

For convenience, the range of each part may be classified

under three headings: level or conversational, traditional, and extreme. In Example 1 are indicated the ranges within which singers are entirely comfortable. Music written in such a limited vocal area may continue indefinitely without producing physical fatigue. The ranges given in Example 2 are those which singers traverse in the course of the average choral composition. Each part has a compass which allows ample melodic expansion, yet which does not subject the performer to vocal strain. Example 3 represents the extremes of range beyond which it is generally inadvisable to venture. For textual reasons

or where the music is fortissimo, the upper limits may occasionally be raised. But such excursions should be, at most, of brief duration. Similarly, in pianissimo writing, higher notes than those indicated may be obtained by the use of the falsetto voice. These notes, however, involve some knowledge of voice-placement usually outside the attainments of the choral singer. On the other hand, in the case of sizeable groups there is an unexplainable choral competence which enables the individual as a part of the mass to accomplish what would be almost impossible for him when singing alone. For this reason the composer should not discard as impractical the writing of high pianissimo passages. The tenor part in Example 4, though it has been creditably sung by amateurs, was obviously intended to be vocal "chamber music" performed by expert singers.[1]

In cases where a high note is manifestly beyond the range

[1] The number at the right of the title of each illustration indicates the page of the work in which that illustration is found. For the edition used, consult the Index of Compositions.

of the average choralist, a second choice is generally provided. In Example 5 the first alto would normally be assigned to the second soprano, the choice of *A* flat or *C* in the first sopranos being dictated purely by vocal capacity. The composer hopes, of course, that in performance the division of parts will remain as indicated, but the wise choral writer leaves as little as possible to chance. The high soprano *C* is a climax note and Holst

has prepared it by a two-beat rest before the penultimate *G*. The *C* occurs but once, it is followed by more than two measures in which the chorus is silent, and it does not lie in a field of consistently high notes. In short, the composer, realizing that he is asking for a supreme though brief effort on the part of the singers, has dealt humanely with them. Far different is Example 6 which may not hold the record for altitude, but which certainly surpasses any test of vocal endurance of which the author has knowledge.

To go below the bottom notes as given in Example 3 may mean loss of timbre, and, in the case of the basses, a blurring of pitch, a scratchy tone, and even the complete abandonment of vocal effort. Almost every chorus has a few unusually high or low voices, and certain geographical areas are noted for possessing these in number. One of the idiomatic effects possible to Russian choruses results from the possession by their contrabasses of such notes as appear in Example 7.

Rarely are sopranos called upon to sing below their range, and the low *A* at the end of the next example is useful chiefly as a means of allowing the sopranos to complete their phrase (Ex. 8).

The sustained note in Example 9 would, of necessity, be given to tenors in most cases. Few choruses can command even one alto capable of producing an *E* below middle *C,* to say nothing of four such unusual voices. The note, if it occurred in the midst of a passage, might be attainable by a very few singers, but as the first note of the phrase it becomes doubly hazardous. Furthermore, as there are twenty tied measures of this *E,* relays would have to be employed; and with only four voices it would be difficult to conceal the vocal entrances and exits of the performers.

For writing in more than four parts, when a single part is treated *divisi,* or when a phrase or a whole composition is designed for men's or women's voices exclusively, the *tessitura* is subject to still further subdivision [2] (Ex. 10).

The reader will note that the sum of the ranges of the first and second sopranos is equal to the total range of the soprano part given in Example 3, and that observation is true of all the parts excepting the bass, where the range of the first bass, or baritone, exceeds by one half step the total range of the bass voice. This is due to the fact that the quality of the bass section in the upper region of the *tessitura* is subject to fluctuation depending on the relative number of first and second basses taking part. If it is desired to carry the baritones up beyond *E* flat, then *F* or even *F* sharp will be found to be preferable to E natural which is a difficult note for chorus baritones to convert into good tone. To write above *D* for a group of baritones and basses combined is to invite forcing by the low basses with a resulting coarseness in quality.

It would not be possible to catalogue the manifold ways in which voices may be grouped.[3] Seldom does any one method persist for long, and within the space of a few measures several

[2] The idea that the second soprano, second alto, etc., are voices somewhat lower than the first soprano and first alto belongs to harmonic rather than to contrapuntal thinking. Before the nineteenth century vocal polyphonists when employing two soprano parts in the course of a work generally appear to have written without regard to range. Nowadays, however, especially in harmonic style, "second" voices are confined to a lower range.

[3] The term "voice grouping" implies an arbitrary arrangement of notes according to harmony. By far the greater part of choral music, however, is contrapuntal, so the term must be taken as defining a principle rather than a practice. It is true, of course, that in harmony one *groups* the voices, whereas in counterpoint one *distributes* them. Fundamentally, the method for both, as far as such questions of range and spacing are concerned, is uniform. That method may most easily be demonstrated by harmony; hence the selection of the term "voice grouping."

types of grouping may occur. Furthermore, when voice-crossing is employed, a single part may be led into the upper or lower reaches of its range without changing the spatial aspect of the voice arrangement, only the choral color being affected.

Four-part writing is the normal medium, and within it there are eight master groupings or methods of voice distribution which are dominant in choral practice and which merge in endless combinations. Of these, six are "range" groupings; that is, they are named according to the range in which each voice is found. The other two are "space" groupings, taking their character from the distance which separates the voices.

The first type (Exs. 11 and 12) confines the voices to the normal or conversational range. For obvious reasons this

method is not maintained for long; but it is often a telling resource in cases where the text implies monotony or a certain intensity of feeling. In the ninety-five measures of Palestrina's *Improperia* the bass is occasionally separated from the soprano by as much as two octaves; but generally the distance is not greater than a twelfth. The soprano never exceeds the range of a fifth, the alto of a sixth, the tenor of a sixth, and the bass of a tenth. The skill of sixteenth-century composers, in particular, in writing contrapuntally within a limited compass is witnessed by the large amount of choral music "for equal voices" belonging to that period. Much of this is in three parts, though four are sometimes employed. Such music may be sung, with only a change of key, by men's voices, women's voices, or a mixture of the two. There results from narrow range and from rhythmic monotony (the *Improperia* is in "familiar style") an almost hypnotizing insistence, so that the hearer feels that each reproachful question is being put directly to him. Such a restricted grouping may, on the other hand, occasionally be used for purely musical reasons, as in the Tschaikowsky excerpt (Ex. 11). In most cases, however, the long maintained continuance of a uniform color or range is likely to irritate both singer and listener.

The second grouping, Examples 13 and 14, embraces the ranges given in Example 2. This may be called orthodox group-

ing as it involves no excursions into the field of special effect, either by the voices individually or in combination. It occurs far more often than any other type of grouping.

Third is the arangement of all the voices in high position.[4]

[4] It has not been thought useful to break down the various ranges into categories more precise than may be indicated by the terms "high" and "low." An inspection of

Climaxes, brilliant endings, and fortissimo passages are often set according to this formula (Exs. 15, 16).

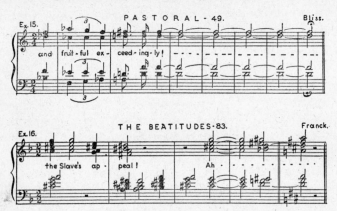

There is a strained quality in the upper part of the range of the amateur voice, which, if judiciously used, may be an effective means of suggesting emotional tension, pleading, aspiration, pathos, or kindred feeling (Exs. 17, 18).

Texts suggesting height are most obviously served by their vocal parallel (Exs. 19, 20).

---

the examples will show that the terms are only relative in their significance. Indeed, "high" may mean simply "not low" and "low" mean nothing more than that the voices are not brilliantly placed.

Interesting and unusual uses of high grouping are found in Examples 21 and 22. (For added examples of high grouping see Appendix, Group I.) The type of writing shown in Example 22 is generally beyond the performing power of amateurs,

and in these cases a complete redistribution of the parts is likely to be necessary. A few very high voices may be assigned to the soprano, other first sopranos with second sopranos to the alto, perhaps only altos to the tenor, and tenors and high baritones to the bass. Adjustments of this sort, implying, as they do, a sacrifice of the intended color, are not, of course, necessary when the music is committed to a selected group of professional singers.

The next, and fourth grouping places all the voices in a low register where they are often used in connection with texts of a restful nature [5] (Exs. 23 and 24). This arrangement of

voices is generally marked "piano," but when sung fortissimo it may impart a strong degree of fervor and intensity (Ex. 25).

Just as high grouping often accompanies the idea of exaltation as expressed in the text, so low grouping fulfils a similar function where the composer wishes to portray humility (Ex. 26; see Appendix, Group II; other examples of low grouping are given in the Appendix, Group III). Grief and foreboding find apt conveyance through this method (Exs. 27 and 28).

[5] Both Brahms and Mendelssohn exploited low grouping extensively as a coloristic device, and since their time most skilful choral composers have employed it effectively.

Fifth is the placing of the tenors and basses in a low register, and the sopranos and altos in a high one (Exs. 29 and 30;
see also Appendix, Group IV). Groupings of this kind involving
wide spacing are seldom maintained for long and result most
logically from contrapuntal necessity.

The sixth formula, of frequent occurrence, is the reverse of
the fifth, locating the tenors and basses in the upper section of
their range and the sopranos and altos in a low position (Exs.
31 and 32).

Within this scheme of voice arrangement there is considerable room for flexibility of range without loss of the idiomatic character of the grouping. Aside from the matter of range, the chief requirement is that the voices, especially the tenor and bass, shall lie close together, the maximum of effectiveness being attained by crowding the upper voices down against the lower ones. This grouping may conduce to strong resonance, and if skilfully introduced and manipulated, energizes the music to such an extent that it seems to be electrically charged. Handel was a master of this effect and the tightness and brilliance of his choral scoring owe not a little to his use of this particular method (Exs. 33 and 34; for varied uses of this grouping see Appendix, Group V).

Grouping number seven — the first of the two "space" group-ings — is of comparatively rare occurrence. It places the alto and tenor in the middle and separates them by some distance from the soprano above and the bass below, thus lessening the mutual support upon which the outer voices traditionally de-pend. Perhaps for this reason its use is more frequent in ac-companied than in unaccompanied choral music. In most cases it results from the progress of the individual voices rather than from considerations of color (Exs. 35 and 36 *; see also the Appendix, Group VI).

The eighth and last grouping sets one outer voice apart from all the other voices. An idiomatic employment of this method generally arises either from the melodic wilfulness of the iso-lated voice, or from the composer's desire to accord to either the soprano or bass a particular prominence which may even give it the status of a solo part (Exs. 37 and 38). Obviously

* Copyright in U.S.A. and all countries, 1931, by the Oxford University Press, London.

there are many instances of this grouping in which the melodic element does not figure, when, for example, the bass, as the foundation part, is separated from the tenor by a large interval. Such a case is Example 39. (For further examples of an outer voice separated from the other voices, see Appendix, Group VII.)

These, then, are the eight master groupings into which voices commonly fall. Each is susceptible of modifications without a change of basic classification; but it is obvious that in spite of the most elastic treatment and the most ingenious and varied extension of their possibilities, they all remain, either singly or in combination, monochrome. Indeed, the sharpest differentiation in color of which voices are capable is furnished by setting men's and women's voices in opposition, or as it is sometimes put, contrasting dark with light. Two methods are common: first, that of making a complete and often an abrupt alternation between the higher and lower voices (Ex. 40; for a particularly skilful example of this device the reader is referred to Brahms's

Chorus of Homage); and second, the introduction of one group before the other has finished (Ex. 41; see also the Appendix, Group VIII). Equally simple is the device of interchanging parts, usually with little or no alteration of the harmony (Exs. 42 and 43).

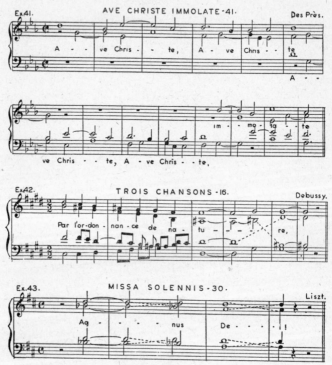

Choral composers, no less than those who write for instruments, may properly look on color as a desirable resource. When an accompaniment is used the problem is not so immediate because the composer may count upon the instrumental part to supply much by way of color that otherwise would be lacking. But it is in *a cappella* writing especially that the opportunity presents itself for a display of skill in the devising of coloristic passages. For this, every conceivable refinement of choral technique is brought into play: the manipulation of the voices, their range, their numerical distribution and their grouping, together with such rhythmic features as will contribute most to the total effect.

Unlike the instrumental composer, the vocal writer must generally wait upon the words to supply the occasion.[6] Sometimes a single word or a brief phrase isolated from the surrounding text, suitable by its suggestion and its sound for coloristic treatment, may be dwelt upon solely for sensuous reasons. Under such circumstances the vocal coda is particularly useful. There, the words having been used up and their meaning fully established, the composer is free to devote himself to the creation of a texture that is for the ear rather than the mind.[7]

The student will rapidly learn how superior is counterpoint to harmony in offering opportunities for the subtle employment of coloristic device. A single voice, even in the course of a moderately extended melody, will take on many changes of quality; and this phenomenon, it should be remembered, is occurring similarly in all the other parts. Furthermore, the inescapable color-pattern set by voices normally grouped with the soprano at the top, then downward through the alto and tenor to the bass is constantly varied by the voice-crossing inevitable in counterpoint. Added to this is rhythmic diversity which may give prominence to a voice that in harmony would be but a subsidiary element in the musical fabric.

[6] The most rational approach to sheer vocal color is, of course, through textless or nearly textless music — a matter which is treated in another connection in Chapter VII.

[7] Among the loveliest of these valedictory passages are those which conclude Byrd's *Justorum Animae, Non Vos Relinquam, Sacerdotes Domini,* and, above all, *Praise Our Lord, All Ye Gentiles.* Beautiful codas also occur in Vaughan Williams' setting of the folksongs *Ca' the Yowes* and *The Turtle Dove;* and the end of Debussy's "Quand j'ai oui le Tabourin," the second of the *Trois Chansons de Charles d'Orléans,* is unsurpassed as choral color.

CHAPTER II

TECHNICAL FUNDAMENTALS

GENERAL CONSIDERATIONS

BEFORE the composer undertakes the double problem of originating musical ideas based on a text and of expressing those ideas in terms of choral writing, he would do well to borrow his melodic material, using it as a point of departure for practice in technical method and in style. For this purpose nothing is more suitable than folksong, a treasure-house of pure melody suggestive of the most varied treatment. In this literature may be found an amazingly large assortment of melodic types. The emotional and substantial differences between the folk tunes of England and Russia, to take but two examples, and the idioms that are as a sea dividing the native music of the Latin countries from its northern prototypes, offer to the student all he might conceivably wish by way of opportunity for practice in the manipulation of vocal material. Indeed, the field of folksong arranging, though not a completely original task, is by no means as circumscribed as it may appear, for in setting, say, a hundred folksongs, one has occasion to employ a very wide variety of technical resource.

As a preliminary to arranging a given melody the student will first have to examine carefully the nature of the tune — whether it best lends itself to harmonic or to contrapuntal treatment or to a combination of both. In the case of certain melodies he may, in the end, decide to withhold his hand entirely, because not all folksongs are susceptible of expansion. Some remain incorrigibly unison or solo, rejecting accompaniment either vocal or instrumental. Others are so "absent-minded" that they defy every intention to reduce them to a logical harmonic basis, or are so self-contained in their beauty that one instinctively recoils from any attempt to add anything to their perfection. But once his folksong is chosen, the arranger should familiarize himself with it by the frequent singing of both music and words; for it is not only the melody, but the text also, which must vitally concern him. At the beginning he will be tempted to omit writing in the words, finding the choral problem sufficient in itself; but this practice is not to be commended, first, because one cannot too early gain a profound sense of the interdependence of words and music,[1] and second, because the text will in many instances suggest the use, in the arrangement or in the instrumental accompaniment, of descriptive devices or of technical means by which the words may be made more significant.[2]

In the same way he should sing the words and music of every voice which he writes as an accompaniment to the given melody. A language sung is not a language spoken, and only by singing may the arranger assure himself of the logical adjustment of the text; by the same means he may also guard against writing voice-parts that are either mechanical or suited primarily to instrumental performance.

It may be said that the best choral writers never confuse the vocal and instrumental issues, not only with regard to the character of their writing, but also in the matter of combining vocal and instrumental resource. Whether or not to use an accompaniment is for them a matter of choice based solely upon the artistic requirements of a particular work. Indeed, one thinks much less of a composer who depends on the support of pianoforte, organ, or orchestra to assist the singers in the performance of a passage which is not vocally conceived. Writing for *a cap-*

[1] Folksongs are a law unto themselves and the fact that there is often a serious discrepancy between the nature of the text and that of the music which accompanies it, and that the same folksong melody is traditionally sung to a number of texts of diverse character, in no way vitiates the fundamental principle in choral composition of the *unity* of words and music.

[2] In this connection see *Swansea Town*, arranged by Holst; *Richard of Taunton Dene*, arranged by G. Williams; and *Dumbarton's Drums*, arranged by Bantock.

pella chorus is, of course, the supreme test of the choral composer's efficiency, and the one which most readily discloses incapacity.[3] Unaccompanied writing for four mixed voices is, then, the field which the student should long cultivate before he undertakes to deal with a larger medium, with special groups, or with accompanied music.[4]

Although the last few decades have revealed the amateur singer's ability to overcome difficulties previously thought insurmountable, with a corresponding increase in the musical vocabulary at the disposal of the composer, the extent to which certain technical features may be used with assurance is still an open question. The composer does not ask, "Can this be sung?" because he may assume that intelligent choristers, with training and experience, can sing anything that is physically possible. What he must guard against is writing music which, though performable, is ineffective; an ineffectiveness due, perhaps, to a vocal psychology that is apparently changeless. One of the disillusionments of the choral composer is the discovery that even a passage in pure diatonic harmony which sounds well when played on the pianoforte and which, by rights, ought to sing easily, will, when committed to the chorus, become painfully discordant. The unalterable fact is that singers are not instruments and they cannot be counted on invariably to perform even a plain succession of non-chromatic intervals with unfailing accuracy.

Beyond the hazards of even simple choral writing stretches the whole area of modern technique with its concepts of melody, harmony, counterpoint, and rhythm, all uniting in a style that is, with most contemporary composers at least, dissonant

---

[3] There is, incidentally, a strong analogy between this type of writing and composition for the string quartet. Lavish and even unskilful orchestration may for the moment impart the semblance of importance to ideas that are feeble, but the composer of the string quartet, restricted as he is to slight instrumental means, must place his reliance first of all upon the significance of what he has to say, and then must set forth his ideas with every technical stroke of which he is master and to the greatest extent that a comparatively limited medium will allow him.

[4] *Divisi*-writing, if attempted at all, should be confined to the final two or three chords where a fuller vocal effect may be desired. The dividing of the parts impinges on the field of polyvocal composition. This style belongs to the higher reaches of choral technique and it is treated in Chapter IV.

in varying degree. Twentieth-century composers have had to face the problem of adapting this style to the field of choral expression, and some have succeeded while others have failed. The successful solutions, by no means uniform or numerous, are, in all cases, based upon the gearing of the composer's individual idiom first to what is friendly to the singer's psychology and second to what, in that idiom, is an effective vocal conveyance of musical ideas. But even if the beginner has, to his satisfaction, formulated as his own an "advanced" musical style, he will yet have much to learn about the physical and mental workings of the singer before he may hope wisely to speak his own language in choral form. Choruses vary widely in the degree of competence they possess, and by and large the composer will do well to observe such restraint in his treatment of material as will leave the average choral group a judicious margin of safety. Folksong will keep him from venturing too far afield, for it is essentially modest music, and is ill at ease in anything but homespun.

Surely the learner normally proceeds from the simple to the complex; and if arranging folk music in orthodox style seems but a pale amelioration of old and chafing technical disciplines, let the student remember that some of the most skilful of modern choral writing exists in the form of folksong settings. In these, as in all expertly conceived vocal music, there abide those fundamental principles in which the greatest choral composers have perennially put their trust.[5]

[5] Folksong settings constitute an important segment of choral literature within which there exists wide diversity of method. The following brief list is representative of the *a cappella* technique of the skilful arranger. Both the harmonic and contrapuntal styles are represented, as well as combinations of both. There are, of course, quantities of settings for men's and women's voices, but only those for mixed chorus are included here. Although they will doubtless be viewed in the main as technical studies, many of them will not fail in artistic impressiveness.

Holst, *I love my love, Swansea Town, Matthew, Mark, Luke and John, There was a tree;* Vaughan Williams, *Ca' the Yowes, Wassail Song, The Turtle Dove, The Lover's Ghost;* Bantock, *Dumbarton's Drums, The Seal Woman's Croon;* Whittaker, *The Captain's Lady;* Mark, *The Birks of Abergeldy-O, O, Will ye gang o'er the Lee Rig?;* Stanford, *Quick, we have but a Second;* Sharp, *The Sheep Shearing;* d'Indy, *Lisette, La querelle d'amour, L'histoire du jeune soldat;* Brahms, *Deutsche Volkslieder* (2 vols.); Rimsky-Korsakoff, *The Spinning-top;* Schindler, *Ballad of the Volga, Down St. Peter's Road.*

HARMONIC SETTINGS

The student will find it advisable in his first essays in the harmonic setting of folksongs to limit himself in each case to a few verses — perhaps not more than three. He may not vary the melody, and the field of harmonic variety consonant with the style of the tune is bound to be comparatively small. He should, therefore, select verses which form a complete narrative or which represent a fully developed idea, and he should, where possible, choose those verses which suggest specific musical treatment. Three forms of arrangement are recommended: first, the setting of all the verses to the same music. This presupposes a highly interesting musical fabric, and probably no marked change of mood in the text of any verse. Although folksongs often pay no attention in the music to emotional changes which take place in the text, the arranger, having in mind the fact that as a composer he must always be on the alert to take account in his music of a shift in the meaning of the words, ought to select verses which are comparatively uniform in import. Second, he may set two of the three verses to identical music, reserving new substance for the third, in most cases, the last. And finally he may, where the text invites it, and where the melody permits such variety, make a different setting for each verse.

The arranger may feel that within these formal patterns he has exhausted every means of making the music interesting, and that even so the total effect when spread over several verses is not sufficiently stimulating. Then he may, providing no violence is done to the meaning of the text, cause one or another of the verses to be sung slower or faster than the others; or he may vary the dynamics, or he may suggest that one verse, let us say, be sung by a solo with choral accompaniment, or by a semi-chorus.

If, at the beginning of his studies, the student is to school himself in obtaining the maximum of variety from limited resource, he should overcome the temptation to resort to counterpoint, but he should, by all means, employ melodic harmony; that is, harmony which pays some attention to the melodic character of the voices. Melodic harmony is not counterpoint, as it does not take into account a long-breathed view of either melody or rhythm. The monotony due to persistent rhythmic coincidence may, however, be lightened in many cases by the use of the dot. Example 44,[6] though strictly harmonic, cannot be said to lack interest. When the dots are removed, however, the whole phrase loses much of its vitality.

Mention has been made of the fact that each line should be native to the singer's art. Now a melody is first of all a succession of intervals, and the arranger should omit those that involve the singer in troubled calculation. Augmented and wide skips have long been current in vocal music, but the singing of them by the amateur is not, even now, the carefree process one might suppose. However, it is preferable to use even doubtful intervals rather than to write a too consistently diatonic line. All intervals through the octave (save augmented ones) and even ninths and tenths are valuable, particularly when they serve to break up the stepwise flow. It is not too much to say that a considerable part of an effectiveness that is primarily choral depends upon the judicious intermingling of skips and diatonic motion. A few demonstrations of the validity of this principle are given (Exs. 45, 46 *, and 47; see also Appendix, Group IX).

The singer's instinct (and it is a sound one) is to turn back

---

* Copyright in U.S.A. and all countries, 1931, by the Oxford University Press, London.

[6] The G naturals in the bass of the third full measure are correct. They are sometimes wrongly given as G sharp.

Ex.45.

O SEIGNEUR, LOUÉ SERA - 9, 10, 11.

Sweelinck.

The great deeds which Thou - - - hast

wrought, the great deeds which Thou hast

- - - wrought, which Thou - - - - - - - - hast wrought

Ex.46.

BELSHAZZAR'S FEAST - 27.

Walton.

And drank wine - - before the thou-sand.

Ex.47.

SYMPHONIE DE PSAUMES - 32, 33.

Stravinsky.

Lau - da - te Do - mi - num, lau - da - te

E - um in cor - dis et or - ga - no;

after making a skip, especially if the interval is fairly large. That instinct, however, is not always to be respected, because a skip may continue in the same direction to form part of an arpeggio, or the second of the two notes may be held long enough to imply a new melodic starting-point. In fact, no rule may be laid down regarding this matter, as the direction pursued by any skip is subject to considerations arising out of the natural logic of the melody and the total choral context.

Voices will often plague the composer by becoming either aimless or static. In the first instance, a sequence, harmonic or rhythmic, or both combined, much as we seem inclined to mistrust it nowadays, will produce at least the verisimilitude of melodic purpose. For the second failing there are a number of remedies. The monotony of a long succession of repeated notes of equal value may be relieved by an octave skip — and this is especially valuable in the bass; by dotting; or by absorbing several of the notes into a longer one, as, for example, three quarter-notes into a dotted half-note.[7]

Again, when two or more successive chords remain in the same harmony, one, and possibly more voices, instead of repeating the same note, may move in arpeggio to form the other notes of the chord.

Among the simpler devices for escaping sluggishness in a vocal line, one has already been mentioned in connection with vocal color, namely, the interchange of notes between two parts (see p. 30). Another is the use of non-harmonic tones including passing-notes, especially accented ones. It goes without saying that these must be melodically significant and not introduced merely to sustain motion. Particularly valuable are suspensions. These, with other non-harmonic factors, create dissonance; and the arranger's taste, prompted by the style of the folksong melody, will determine the extent to which dissonance may be suitably employed. In the harmonic setting of a folk tune, an enterprise which is conditioned on every side

[7] This involves some manipulation of the text, which in itself may add not a little interest to the passage.

by limiting factors, suspensions are, among elementary means of stimulating interest, the most discreet, adaptable, and efficient.

Juggling the notes of a chord in behalf of vocal interest raises the issue as to how far one should go in ignoring the provisions for doubling and spacing laid down in text books on harmony. These provisions are fundamentally sound, but they apply in the main to single chords and therefore they should not be too strictly observed in the writing of melodic vocal harmony. Variety is an essential in choral music and any succession of chords which puts first value on academically correct doubling or spacing does so at the expense of more important considerations. It is generally agreed, for example, that owing to the natural richness of voices, a third written low in a chord tends to produce muddiness of texture. The second of the three chords which constitute the next example, however, though belonging unquestionably to the category of special effects, is unforgettably telling (Ex. 48). This matter of the disposition of thirds

either as regards number or position is one of the refinements of choral writing requiring exceptional care. To say exactly why or under what conditions a doubled third between soprano and bass is valid, for example, would be difficult; one can only state that from the standpoint of choral effect it is among the most valuable assets of the composer. In Example 49 note that the bass *B* (the crucial note) is taken by a leap. But no analysis will reveal how preëminently choral is this touch, and only voices can reveal its true beauty. Beginning with all the voices on the same note (but not necessarily at the same pitch) and doubling the fifth in the opening chord have a peculiar value in that they prepare the way at once for freedom of melodic

Ex.49   ACH LIEBER HERRE JESU CHRIST · 16,17.
Brahms.

progression. The doubling in Example 50 makes possible a three-fold sweep on the syllable "pa" in "pacem." Wide spacing as well as the doubling in Example 51 creates a similar situation. In general, doubling and spacing may be considered subsidiary matters, and unless the student is made aware that the awkward and ill-sounding quality of a succession of chords is due solely to persistent maladjustment, he should seek the cause of the trouble elsewhere.

Ex.50.   MASS IN G MAJOR · 56.   Weber.

STABAT MATER · 45   Rossini.
Ex.51.

In his efforts to employ a fairly wide *tessitura* in each part, the student will properly resort to voice-crossing. But he is advised not to pass above the soprano before the second verse, in order that the given melody may be announced distinctly at least once.[8] Effective crossing of the tenor below the bass is not easy to achieve. Unless the bass is written fairly high the tenor is forced down into an ungrateful range and, in addition, the primarily contrapuntal problem of a false bass arises.

Commendable as are attempts in this simple style to vary

[8] Complete settings of the melody in an inner voice are inadvisable unless a contrapuntal treatment is employed.

range and to gain melodic interest, these should never be gained at the expense of harmonic logic. The harmony must, first of all, be *rational,* and, within that zone of safety, ingenuity must operate as best it can. Rational harmony is that which, within a variable field of choice, fits the character of the melody at every point. The temptation to indulge in frequent harmonic change is admittedly strong. But such composers as Bach and Palestrina created works of length and importance in which amazingly few harmonies were used and in which the same chord persisted throughout a number of measures. Though we have come to think of harmonic reticence with no corresponding lack of eloquence as an exclusive attribute of genius, the beginner will make no mistake, even in such unpretentious efforts as the arrangements of folksongs, if he under — rather than over — exploits harmonic resource.[9] After singing a melody several times the student will begin to sense its implied harmonic rhythm. It may be that the first two or three measures ask for no more than a single harmony, but whatever the harmonic requirements, they must take priority over other considerations.

Although one may think of his harmony in terms of root-position chords, he runs two risks if he uses them consistently. First, the risk of producing uncompromising and exercise-like music, and second, of writing angular and unmelodic basses. Plentiful inversions, especially in the field of seventh chords, are a guard against both dangers.

The mention of seventh chords suggests, of course, the general problem of dissonance as it relates to harmonic choral writing. Until the composer becomes acquainted with the singer's capacity to surmount the difficulties presented by the occurrence in the music of even moderately harsh dissonances, he

[9] In one particular harmonic understatement is not to be encouraged, and that is continuing, except for special reasons, the same chord from a weak beat to a strong one. If, in addition, the bass also is repeated, the diminution of musical interest may be painful. Provided the harmony must remain the same, the bass at least should be changed, and if the bass proves reluctant, then the harmony above it should be altered on the strong beat.

will be well-advised to use preparation. If this is not possible,
the use of the ever-valuable dot will sometimes render the
attack of a sharp discord comparatively easy, or one of the
dissonant factors may be introduced somewhere in the preceding chord. The following case will make both provisions clear.
The omission of the dot at (a) would considerably increase the
difficulty; and the situation at (b) would be greatly complicated
by the substitution of another note for the *E* in the soprano
(Ex. 52). A further safeguard against the danger arising out of

a too brusque attack of dissonance is provided by step-wise
motion in one or both voices. It is when the parts approach the
discord by a leap that the greatest care should be taken. Here
any device which will permit the singers to hear in advance
at least one of the clashing notes is to be recommended and in
any case the skip by which the parts approach each other had
best be by contrary motion. Especially in the opening measures
should dissonance be sparingly used. There also too much or
too involved harmony should be avoided. It must be remembered that at the beginning of a piece there is an unavoidable
tension until the singers have gained their "tonal footing." [10]

Leaving now what may be called the minutiae of technical
procedure, we come to deal with some of the larger aspects of
the harmonic setting of folksongs. First, the motion should
be logical and continuous, preoccupation with harmonic matters never prompting the arranger, save in exceptional cases,
to allow the movement to flag, especially toward the end of a
measure. Furthermore, as many folksongs are regular in phrase-

[10] This admonition is, of course, not so valid in the case of accompanied music
where there may even be an instrumental introduction which establishes the tempo,
the mood and the tonality.

ology, a setting may become hopelessly compartmentalized unless the end of one phrase is now and again fused with the beginning of the next by passing notes or by harmonic continuity. In Example 53 (the melody is in the tenor) the chord at (a) is not cadential; we would expect the tonic in some form rather than the last inversion of the supertonic seventh chord. That chord is the happy result of the arranger's desire to avoid periodicity by employing a long view of the harmony which ignores the phrase-end.

Single groups of short-value notes unless recurring in the same part or elsewhere are stylistically questionable. Increasing activity represented by notes of smaller dimension will often occur as the setting advances. Pace is bound to be a controlling factor in any arrangement and what is effective when slowly sung may sound confused or even incorrect when rapidly performed.

The element of speed is very important where chromatics are in question. Few pieces in the common currency of choral literature are entirely free of chromatics, and those which involve modulation to nearly related keys offer the singers little difficulty, as the modulatory process is familiar to them both as performers and as listeners. At the point in each key-change where chromatics occur, they know what the effect ought to be, and they make such rapid tonal adjustments as may be necessary. The same is true of the oft-used family of altered sixth chords which, even when contrapuntally distributed, are not likely to give rise to faulty intonation. Even though the total pitch of the passage in question may be slightly raised or lowered, the intervals of which it is made up will be relatively true. But once the composer begins to make use of free chromaticism the singer's problems are much more serious. An amateur vocalist with a well-trained ear may perform his part alone with moderate success, and he may even perform two or three conjunct altered intervals accurately; but when he sings his part with others all of whom are in like case, there is a loss of corporate confidence; it is each man for himself; and the result is more often than not complete tonal anarchy. Until the composer learns how far it is wise to venture in the direction of chromatic writing he is advised to use alterations sparingly and to be sure that each voice represents a tonal thread; that is, that each part is a melody capable of harmonization by itself and that the chromatics it contains are such as might normally occur in the course of that melody. Even these precepts, however, cannot be viewed as invariable. There is probably no detail of choral composition which presupposes as much firsthand experience with voices as does the writing of chromatics. Here are two excerpts, both of which are extremely chromatic; and though both have certain details in common, only one of the two passages is really practicable. Both examples employ sequences which are, to be sure, definitely helpful to singers in any musical circumstances which tend to be chaotic. But Example 54 employs sequence only in the upper voice, while Example 55 sets a pattern in all the parts. Furthermore, each of the parts in Example 55 is susceptible of a harmonization which emphasizes tonic and dominant chords sufficiently to orient the singers in the successive keys through which they progress. Example 54, on the other hand, represents for the greater part only a segment of the chromatic scale, which is a perennial vocal pitfall. And last, Example 54, already unnaturally difficult, must be sung without instrumental support; while Example 55 provides an accompaniment which doubles

the voices at every point. (For further examples of chromatic choral style see Appendix, Group X.)

Italian tunes, both true folksongs and tunes of the popular type, either by their inclusion of altered notes or because of their character, often invite chromatic treatment. Their nature frequently suggests a harmonization that is leisurely, and the chromatics may be handled in the same manner. These should be spread out over each voice so that there is no concentration at one point leading to doubtful intonation. Vocal music which moves quickly is not friendy to chromaticism, and successively altered notes, whether in a single part or appearing simultaneously in several voices, when performed allegro are likely to give rise to difficulties. Fortunately both the text and music of many Italian tunes are unsuited to rapid performance.

The harmonization of purely diatonic melodies, however, should with very rare exceptions remain faithful to the notes of the scale to which those melodies belong.[11] Melodies in the minor mode, in particular, offer the arranger considerable chromatic scope. Both the sixth and the seventh of that mode appear in an altered and an unaltered form and considerable variety is possible through the use in *A* minor, for example, of *F* natural and *F* sharp, *G* natural and *G* sharp scattered throughout the harmonization. Sixteenth-century composers, particularly in England, were fond of chromatic conflict and succeeding generations of choral writers have capitalized on the principle. Examples 56, 57, and 58 display varying uses of this principle. (See also Appendix, Group XI.)

The factors which determine the choice of key vary somewhat depending on whether the medium is to be accompanied or unaccompanied. In the latter case the composer is inclined to

[11] Modal tunes should be even more strictly confined to the substance of their modes.

be fatalistic, for he knows that the conductor will often, either from caprice or necessity, select a key other than that in which the piece is written; and that if the conductor does not elect to exercise this prerogative, the chorus will, in many cases, do it for him. But the composer will hope for the best and he will plan his key mainly with two issues in mind: first, the atmosphere or mood which he wishes to be dominant in the work; and second, he will look forward to those parts of the piece where he desires to create the greatest impression by his treatment of the words. It sometimes happens that he will work out a few phrases in which the arrangement of the voices is exactly what the text requires; each voice traverses the right range and the grouping or distribution gives just the effect he has in mind. Then he may, if this is the focal point of his piece, plan to begin in a tonality which will allow the inclusion of this particular section as it stands.[12] If it is the final cadence, and particularly the final chord, on which the arranger is intent, he may, provided the chorus sings the piece at the given pitch, count on certain keys to produce the desired result. The student may find it useful to write out a series of cadential formulae, V–I and IV–I, which would yield a maximum of resonance, always remembering that the grouping employed for the penultimate chord, and the ability of the bass to go up rather than down at the end, play a large part in the transaction. But far more useful will be a close study of the method used by composers whose cadential climaxes are models of brilliance, noting, in addition, how much their manipulation of the material preceding the climax affects the final result. The student will certainly discover, among other details, that it is skilful, rather than merely high grouping, which is most rewarding.[13]

The arrangement of the words throughout the music is

---

[12] The same group of notes will sometimes recur a number of times in the course of a folksong melody, and where the arranger has evolved several different settings for the same melodic group, he should try to introduce them in the order of their interest, saving the most stimulating for the last.

[13] For examples of chords brilliantly scored see Chapter I, pp. 23, 24, and Group I in the Appendix.

taken up in subsequent pages, and no more than four elementary matters need be mentioned here. First, unaccented syllables should not fall upon accented places in the measure. Second, the distribution of the text must conform to the requirements of "singers' speech," and what is natural for the

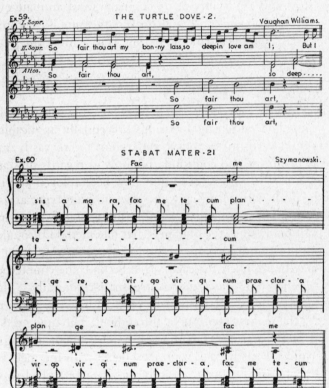

singer can only be discovered by actual test. Third, even moderately rapid articulation by the sopranos or tenors in a high range, or basses in a low one, should be avoided. Fourth, in order to vary the uniformity of word arrangement, throughout all the parts, the singing of the same words with notes of varying value is recommended. In Example 59, while the sopranos sing "So fair thou art my bonny lass, so deep in love am I," the other parts give out the first four words twice in augmentation. Diminution of text is also available (Ex. 60). In arranging folk melodies it is not enough to write good music, for in such a case the arranger may do no more than produce a succession of beautiful choral sounds. The meaning of the text and the beauty of its language must animate every musical intention and must vitalize every measure if the composition, even a simple harmonic setting, is to achieve the stature of a work of art.

Contrapuntal Settings

Many of the principles stated in connection with the harmonic method of setting folksongs are equally applicable to contrapuntal treatment; but counterpoint offers vastly more by way of variety and continuity not only as regards substance, but form as well. More verses may now be employed and they may be dealt with in divers ways.[14] Seven main types are suggested, a number of which may be incorporated in a single composition. Indeed, the pursuit of but one method throughout an entire piece might result in monotony. First, a different setting may be supplied for each verse. Second, the counterpoint may be relieved by one or more verses set harmonically.[15] Third, rests, pauses, or interludes may be omitted between the verses, making the melody continuous throughout. The tune need not persist in the soprano, but may be handed about among the other voices. Fourth, each verse may be set with the melody in a different part. Fifth, the melody may be overlapped so that one verse begins before another has ended. Sixth, the tune may be ascribed in one or more verses to a solo voice, the remainder

[14] Where several verses are used, an occasional substitute may be found for the tonic triad as the harmony for the initial note of the melody. Numbers of tunes, furthermore, are adapted, in their earlier measures, to either a major or a minor harmonization; thus if verse one begins in the major, verse two may employ the minor in the opening phrase.

[15] In general the progress should be from harmony to counterpoint unless the text strongly justifies the reverse procedure. Once the contrapuntal style has been established, a reversion to harmony, except incidentally, will almost certainly mean a falling off in interest.

of the chorus being used as an accompaniment. The supporting parts may have words, but the solo will be more characteristically individual if the words are in some places, at least, adjusted differently from those of the solo. If words are not given to the chorus, humming or vocalization on some vowel may be used. Seventh, the material of the melody or substance germane to the melodic idea may be developed to form articulating joints between the verses. This practice may be extended to include brief vocal preludes and codas.

Of these seven methods, some, at least, presuppose the placing of the melody elsewhere than in the soprano; but as few folk melodies furnish a satisfactory bass, the choice will generally fall either to the alto or tenor. Placing the melody of a folksong in an inner voice materially increases the arranger's difficulties. Let us assume that the tune has been in the soprano, allowing the bass to receive the bulk of melodic care. Now, however, the tune is in a subsidiary part and though attention presumably will focus on it, nevertheless both bass and soprano, as the outer and most prominent voices, must not be allowed to lose their melodic importance. The soprano especially must vie in interest with the given melody, but must not rival its preëminence.[16] The folksong itself must stand out clearly, and this, admittedly, presents a problem, but one which may be solved in one of four ways or by a combination of them. First, the tune being in an inner voice, the number of accompanying parts should be reduced, especially at the beginning, to one or, at most, two; or the melody may even be allowed to stand alone for a few measures. Later, three parts, if judiciously written, may occasionally be employed. Second, when the chief melody is in motion, the accompanying parts may remain static or nearly so. This principle is particularly applicable to tunes which are melodically and rhythmically active. Third, the rhythm of the secondary parts should generally be contrary

[16] An occasional sequence will do much to bolster up the melodic self-respect of a soprano or any other part that threatens to become merely a succession of accompanying notes.

to and not coincident with that of the given tune. And fourth, should there be any question of the audibility of the chief melody, the arranger may double that voice by another.

The distribution of the melody by sections among the various voices is a delicate manoeuvre. Clearly the thread of the tune must never be lost, and to this end many of the suggestions in the foregoing paragraph are pertinent. It is mainly in stylistic adjustment that difficulties arise. Here, for example, is an alto which suddenly drops its rôle of accompanying voice, becomes, for the moment, the chief personality in the play, and then as precipitately is again merely a subsidiary character. Such a dilemma would give pause to a skilful dramatist, and for the musician the puzzle is no less formidable. The transitions, of course, must not be too abrupt, and the part must remain "in character" throughout; otherwise it will not be convincing as a stylistic unit. The partitioning of the melody among the voices is often a not too commendable technical tour de force; it is justified, however, when the tune embraces a range too wide to be covered by any one part; or when the range is so limited as to make a change of color desirable.

Each of the seven suggested methods of setting folksongs contrapuntally implies a measure of calculation, but the seventh, involving the writing of interlocking joints, is the most highly organized of all and demands both ingenuity and constructive skill. Before reaching the end of a verse, the arranger should decide which voice is next to take up the melody. That voice should conclude at some point prior to the close of the verse, so that when it reënters its significance as the bearer of the chief melody will be emphasized. The principle of calling attention to a single part by the preliminary introduction of a pause has been well known since mediaeval times, and its validity is in no wise lessened today.

Of the joints themselves, as of all interlocutory phrases, one definite requirement may be made. These must not sound like improvisations, but must be so invariably spontaneous and so coördinated with the rest of the music as to give the impression that they are no less a part of the work than the verse itself. Although short imitative matter will often be useful, it should never be simply a demonstration of technical cleverness, but should be an inevitable outgrowth of the style.

The particular value of writing connecting sections (joints) between the verses of a folksong is that for the moment the arranger is working without benefit of cantus and must rely mostly on his own originality for the result. The main material at his disposal will naturally be that which he draws from the tune, and his own original contributions should have due regard for this fact. He may, however, go beyond that principle. If, let us say, the structure of the melody falls in regular phrases of four measures each, he can make a telling contrast by casting his interlude in the form of a five- or seven-measure phrase. Beyond such simple excursions, however, he should hesitate to venture lest he become involved in matter contrary to the implied style. In particular he should think well before employing modulation unless this is a feature of the melody itself, and if it is he is probably not dealing with pure folksong. But if the tune inclines to monotony, both in itself and in its suggested harmony, and if the arranger is forced to use a goodly number of verses, he may, if the setting is predominantly harmonic, end his verse in one key and begin the next in a nearly related tonality. If the setting is contrapuntal he will probably proceed to the new key by a transitional modulation incorporated into the interlude. In that case care should be taken that the chromatics are introduced as inconspicuously as possible, namely on weak rather than on strong beats, and melodically rather than harmonically. Sometimes the arranger will wish to set a verse for women's or men's voices only and he will find that the original key does not accommodate itself to this idea. Modulation is then the only solution. Modulation, furthermore, may be necessary to bring the melody within a range suitable to the voice — perhaps an inner one — to which it is given. But on the whole, change of key should be a last resort and every other means of creating interest should first be exploited.

Continuity is destroyed and the interlude becomes a mere intrusion between the verses if the hearer is made aware of the points at which the transition begins and ends. In avoidance of this the ideal type of interlude is that which overlaps the final measures of one verse and the initial measures of the next. The following graph will illustrate this method.

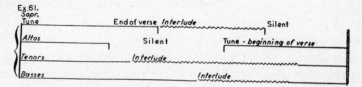

The above scheme is intended to be merely typical. It represents one possible approach; but its application, even as it stands, is manifold. Though no rests or slightly longer pauses are indicated, they are, naturally, almost inevitable in the music. Four details may be observed: first, the preparation, by silence, of the alto as the main melody; second, the withdrawal, after the new verse has begun, of the soprano, the voice upon which the chief interest has up to this point been fastened and from whose particular color the ear may reasonably be temporarily relieved; third, the limiting of the number of the voices accompanying the new verse; and fourth, the unerring continuity of the music.

Here is a really beautiful example of a joining passage (Ex. 62).

The writing of connective passages, like other technical matters yet to be considered, relates chiefly to restricted segments of the music. What the arranger must remember is that one of his main concerns will be the integrating of the counterpoint as a whole. Therefore, in making what adjustments are necessary in the interests of clarity and effectiveness at any one point, he must see to it that the total counterpoint is marked by logical continuity. The most frequent compromise that will be necessary will be for the purpose of preserving the sense of the harmonic background. But this composers have been doing for centuries and the arranger will be able to estimate his competence in no small degree by the extent to which he sustains harmonic propriety without disturbing the naturalness of the contrapuntal flow.[17]

Up to this point melody has been treated largely as a succession of intervals. Thus the arranger was warned that in writing the accompanying voices he must be wary of equivocal melodic progressions, of a too limited range, and of static areas. Contrapuntal writing, however, implies an extended view of melody. Long held notes, or even successive repeated notes, are often desirable as a contrast, or may be employed provided their use is native to the character of the melody.[18] Melodic concentration must now be on two details: first, the *style of the melody* and second, its *vocality*. Each accompanying voice must be a reflection of the given tune. It must, itself, be susceptible of harmonization; though its physiognomy may not greatly resemble that of the parent melody, and though there will almost certainly be a disconcerting gulf between the individuality and charm of the two, their natures must, nonetheless, be distinctly akin.

Of all the accompanying parts the bass will be the most troublesome, because in unaccompanied choral writing he must play a double rôle. He is at once the foundation of the implied harmony, and, at the same time, a melody in his own

[17] This problem is far more easily dealt with in polyvocal and in accompanied writing where either because of the presence of more than four parts or of an additional bass supplied by the accompaniment, harmonic stability may be maintained without jeopardizing the melodic independence of the various voices.

[18] See Chapter III, pp. 76, 78, 79, 80, 81, for material on this subject.

right. The bass and soprano traditionally bear the melodic burden; and though the bass for reasons of style may be much more of a bass than a melody, he is at his best when he is a combination of both.

It is in facing the problem of vocality that the student will probably first discover that his previous training in the theoretical branches of music must be extended to include a new element. Melodies which satisfy the rules or which are suited to instrumental performance may be far from the singer's ideal. Vocality may best be described as "what the singer loves to do." It is related not only to the melismatic or extended treatment of a single vowel, but applies as well to the whole melody from the first note to the last. In the sixteenth century vocality was, naturally, the essence of the melodic line. Example 63 is a section of the tenor part of a motet by Tallis. This represents

the sixteenth-century ideal of vocality as English composers in particular expressed it. A later and unsurpassed demonstration of opulence in the vocal line is this passage from Mozart's *Great Mass in C Minor* (Ex. 64).

Vocality in choral as in solo writing often takes the form of spreading the voices over several measures without change of vowel. This is the very life of vocal expansion; the opportunity which the singer enjoys and which is intrinsic in vocal art. The eighteenth century especially cultivated it, but numerous citations from every choral era could be offered (Ex. 65).

Such vocality as is demonstrated in the foregoing examples is to be found only in the works of those composers who have perceived and respected the particular nature of the singing voice and those who employ it. A composite made up of gift, insight, training, and experience, the power to write true "singers' music" is not easily gained; but the student should court it ardently if he wishes to be a choral composer in all that those words imply.

As far as is consonant with other considerations, each line must be *given its head*. All melodies which are worthy of the name have a destiny which is forecast in the first phrase and consummated in the last; and this is not less true of the inner voices so often unduly sacrificed for larger musical interests.[19] Each voice which accompanies a folksong is a musical personality and no blanket recommendations, therefore, may be made regarding its treatment; but there will be in every melody certain crucial notes whose location should provoke thought. These are the notes which cap the melody at various points and which are normally, but not invariably, graded upward by gentle degrees, reaching a clamax at some point near the end. A melody which displays its peak too soon runs the risk of being anticlimatic.[20]

As the harmonic settings which the student makes may be

[19] The author realizes that he risks the accusation of committing at least mild sacrilege; nonetheless he ventures to suggest that every young contrapuntist should hopefully memorize the sixth verse of the 51st Psalm: "Behold, thou desirest truth in the inward parts: And in the hidden part thou shalt make me to know wisdom."

[20] Climax notes are, in a sense, "effect-notes," and are more striking when approached by a skip.

viewed as practice in the simple use of choral material rather than as essays in choral style, little mention of rests has thus far been made; but these are no less than idiomatic in choral writing. Singers must breathe and must be given intermittent intervals of repose. Choral conductors are justly suspicious of any piece which does not appear to be cast in "open-work" style; and they are often forced to reshuffle the text in the interest of a more humane arrangement; [21] but to the composer to whom text distribution is an integral part of choral writing, the committing of this important feature to the conductor's care will not commend itself.

Rests, moreover, are effective in removing periodically one or more voices from the texture, voices whose reappearance is doubly welcome even after a brief absence. Phrase logic, too, is materially assisted by pauses, but passages separated by rests must make both their departure and their reëntrance in a completely natural manner, and this is not merely a question of the music, but of the text as well. It would be impossible to make too much of this matter which concerns one of the most serious pitfalls besetting the choral composer. The vertical aspect of his music will be close to his thought; and discovering that the alto, perhaps, has been deprived of rests for an unreasonable length of time, he will seek out a place where her momentary withdrawal will cause no undue thinning of the texture. But he may then find that the alto takes her departure in a very awkward musical way, or that no sensible adjustment of the text may be made in the phrase which precedes her rest. Each line, then, must be considered apart from the harmony. Example 66 is a particularly happy illustration of how rests may set off one phrase from another, each quite self-contained, both musically and textually.

Example 66 does more, however, for it embodies seven additional points which are important. First, the writing is un-

[21] Bach, in writing choral roulades, was quite indifferent to breathing places, and the only means by which a forte may be sustained in his long florid passages is by frequent and haphazard breathing.

Ex.66. HERZLIEBSTES BILD - 3,4. Hofhaimer.

mistakably contrapuntal without abandoning a harmonic basis that is rational. The student may, indeed, find it interesting to determine which of the four parts is the main melody. This, moreover, is essentially *vocal* counterpoint, mingling steps and skips in due proportion and singing with perfect ease and naturalness. Second, the distribution of the rhythm in any single voice or in all the voices taken together represents a high degree of ingenuity which must lead to sustained interest on the part of both singers and listeners.[22] Third, the accentuations of the text are repeated in the music. Reference to such an elementary and self-evident fact may appear quite unnecessary; the truth is, however, that not only beginners, but sometimes experienced composers as well, commit the unforgivable sin against common sense of allowing an unaccented syllable of text to coincide with a strong musical beat. Example 67, for instance, is very faulty. The last syllable of "waiting" should not fall on the first beat of the measure; as with all present participle

---

[22] Not a little of the effectiveness in some sections of César Franck's choral works is due to the maintenance of a diversified rhythm simultaneously in all the parts.

endings, only one or two notes should accompany it, and the bottom *F* is certainly too low for the average alto.

Fourth, in Example 66 no unimportant word or syllable is accorded a position of importance in the melody. Two examples (68 and 69) of a disregard of this principle are offered.

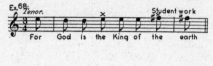

Fifth, the change from word to word, or syllable to syllable, as shown in Example 66, is quite normal. One of the most vexing difficulties for the beginner is to accomplish these changes at points in the melody where they seem inevitable. Examples 70 and 71 clearly indicate that the results were never put to trial.

Sixth, again in Example 66, where musical circumstances dictate the repetition of bits of text, or the reordering of the words, the sense remains complete in spite of alteration. Beginners, having ordained (generally for harmonic reasons) that the phrase shall end at a certain point, and finding themselves

in difficulties with regard to the adjustment of the text, will
often cast meaning to the winds provided they supply the
singers with some sort of verbal vehicle. Example 72 is an inner
voice taken from student work. A natural conclusion to the

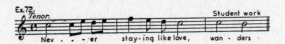

phrase would be two quarter rather than half notes. The text is
"Never staying, like love it wanders"; but there being no place
in the composer's music for "it," that important word is
omitted with all too evident solecistic results. Similarly the
words "a custodia matutina usque ad noctem" mean nothing
when foreshortened as in Example 73. Seldom, in contrapuntal

writing, will the entire text be present in all the voices; parts
that are silent for a time are presumably listening to the text as
it is sung by the others, and at an appropriate moment they
may, as in conversation, join with the others at any given point.
But each phrase should, by itself, make sense. Seventh, at (a),
(b), and (c) in the alto part of Example 66 the composer has
solved one of the most vexing of minor choral problems, namely
the adjustment of the text on a repeated note. Suppose, for
example, that he had set the passage (Ex. 66) at (a) in this
manner as inexpert craftsmen often do (Ex. 74). In that case

the singer is forced to articulate distinctly the two *G*'s on the
same monosyllabic word. If that is to be done he must sing
"wi-hill" which, while an entirely reputable device of vocal
technique, is, under the circumstances, laborious. He might

have tied the two *G*'s together, but a shorter note tied to a longer is certainly more disturbing to the vocalist than to the instrumentalist. Or he might have proceeded as in Example 75 which makes the octave skip an uncomfortable operation. In addition, two general observations may be made. A rapid diatonic passage which repeats its final note is difficult to sing, and the second of two repeated and fairly rapidly articulated notes is most easily performed when the syllable which accompanies it begins with a moderately percussive consonant as in Example 75.

Awkward handling of repeated notes is but one of the discomforts which the unskilful composer may inflict on the singers. Others more nearly affect the music itself. For instance, among equivocal dissonant uses, none needs more to be put to the test of actual performance than the unison approached stepwise. Effective as it is in instrumental music, its variability in choral writing is so great that unless its value in a specific case is proved by actual performance it is often wisest to consummate the approach at the octave rather than the unison. That, at least, is the counsel of safety. There are possible, I believe, no categorical recommendations regarding this device. When expertly handled it results in effects of great beauty. On the whole, the unison approached stepwise appears to be at its best when not low in the *tessitura,* when occurring in the course of contrapuntal motion, either passing through or turning back from the unison, when the union is effected by a whole rather than a half-step, when the interval of the second is approached stepwise, when the approaching note is not held just before it takes the unison, when the stationary note has been sustained for a time before the unison takes place, or when the merging of the two notes is not accompanied by a change of harmony. Example 76 demonstrates a highly successful use of the unison approached stepwise. In this example there is a distinct congestion of the voices at (a), (b), and (c) producing extraordinary vocal richness; but not always is the result so happy. (For various approaches to this problem see Appendix, Group XII.)

The assembling or crowding together of voices on adjacent degrees of the scale is usually a brief occurrence arising from contrapuntal motion, and is often compensated for by a passage scored in correspondingly wide spacing. A rare instance of voice-crowding in a long-held coloristic effect is presented in Example 77 written for double chorus. Holst, whose broad experience made him keenly sympathetic to the frailties of choral singers, frequently gathered all the voices on a unison or an octave either as a point of departure for a dissonant chord or as a rallying ground after the chord had been quitted.

Special groupings like those just mentioned will sometimes find their way into the music because the composer is preoccupied with the abstract technical problem rather than with the choral issue. In the same way, having begun with four voices he will continue to the end thinking in terms of four-part harmony or counterpoint. No more valuable principle could be urged upon the student than that of the periodic reduction in the number of voices. Failing a conscientious observance of that precept the composer will speedily weary both performers and audience. The normal beginning is in four parts, but if the full number is not used it is well to let a single voice enter, then each of the others in turn; or two voices may begin followed by the remaining two. The least successful formula is to begin with one voice and then to bring in the other three simultaneously.[23]

How important to the choral composer is a "less-than-four-part" technique may be gathered from a study of the choral music of an earlier day. The wisdom of fifteenth- and sixteenth-century musicians is nowhere more clearly attested than in their frequent employment of the three-part grouping. Here there was, in many cases, no need of doubling, and each note of every voice possessed an unique individuality.[24]

While a reduction in the number of voices, whether temporary or fixed throughout the composition, is an aid to clarity, it is quite as often invoked by composers as a means of underlining the text. In the same way that a particularly trenchant musical idea may lose its power when cast in involved contrapuntal language, so a text that is dramatic or poignant may be most forceful when accompanied by only one or two lines of music. The words are of first importance and the composer is frequently unwilling to allow even the ordinary four-part choral texture to distract attention from their significance.[25]

Unison writing is more effective than that in octaves, though the latter device is often valuable as a melodic reinforcement. Thus, if the soprano has the main melody, and for some reason the arranger wishes to call particular attention to it, he may double it an octave lower in the tenor, for example. Impressive orchestral sonority may be gained by limiting the writing to octaves, but just the reverse is true of choral method. Beethoven constantly miscalculated in this particular as the number of his

[23] Other factors being equal, the composer, if the choice is his, will generally introduce an entering voice on a weak beat.

[24] Examples of two- and three-part writing may be found in the choral collection entitled *Laudate Pueri,* edited by Tovey.

[25] For a striking example of the application of the principle of part-reduction to instrumental writing, see the pianoforte score of Debussy's *Pelléas et Mélisande,* pp. 215–217. These pages seem remarkable chiefly for their frugality. To understand how transcendently the intensity of the drama is illuminated by the music in all particulars recourse must be had to the orchestral score at this point.

ineffective vocal climaxes will show. On the other hand, two, three, and, where possible, four voices singing in unison are capable of much dynamic power; and at a point where the significance of the text is best helped by no sharing of the interest with polyphony, the most impressive rendering is often by means of unison, or, if necessary, octave writing.

There is another and quite different use for the single concerted vocal line, and that is under circumstances which suggest the employment of a solo voice, but where the composer's ends are best served by calling on all the voices of a single part. There are certainly sections of text so full of meaning that they ask to be rendered as personally as possible. If they are long enough, and the work is accompanied, they are generally scored for a solo voice; where they are not, they are best given to all the voices of one part. How impressive unison or octave writing may be when used to underscore the text will appear from an examination of Examples 78 and 79 (see also Appendix, Group XIII).

Example 80 shows a doubling of the bass and soprano two octaves apart.

The arrangement of the voices in two strands is common where, again, a thinning out of the texture is desired. Often as in Example 82 the voices are moved alternately (see also Appendix, Group XIV).

Numerous passages occur in which one doubled voice is accompanied by two others (Ex. 83; see also Appendix, Group XV).

For even greater emphasis, one of the two voices is sometimes tripled (Ex. 84; see also Appendix, Group XVI).

Orchestral composers are familiar with the difference between "paper" music and "heard" music. Neatly planned passages for stopped horns or an apparently impressive figure for the clarinet are, when played, sometimes submerged in a mass of corollary material. For the choral composer these mishaps occur quite as often as otherwise in his handling of the element of dissonance. Dissonant effects which look convincing and which sound so when played on the pianoforte are frequently unprofitable when sung. It is by no means always possible to explain these failures. They may be due to the fact that the place in the range where the discord occurs is not favorable for the voices to which the dissonance is assigned; but one cannot doubt that a large proportion of unsuccessful vocal dissonances miss fire simply because they are dealt with too briefly. One of the truly magnificent strokes at the command of the choral composer is resounding dissonance; but any discord must have a certain amount of leisure for making itself fully articulate. Some care must be expended, of course, in the approach; but far more is necessary once the dissonance has begun to sound and at the moment of resolution. Much, but not all, will depend on tempo. Dissonances rapidly attacked, as rapidly quitted and placed on weak beats, are seldom good. If such a use is necessary, a line (but never an accent) placed under the note on which the dissonance falls will indicate to the singer that he must take particular pains to make the required effect. The result is likely to be even less satisfactory if, in resolving the discord, the performer sings a new word or syllable. Sometimes a consonant or even two must be enunciated by the singer before the vowel which makes the dissonance audible is reached ("*W*ill" or "*sh*all"). Under these circumstances the dissonance may hardly be heard at all and may seem to have little connection with its resolution, the whole process giving the impression that the singer has missed his note.[26] Even when

[26] Experiment has proved that apparent harmonic confusion as well as ineffective dissonance is beneficially affected by substituting a single syllable or monosyllabic word for a passage involving even a moderate amount of articulation. Vowel continuity uninterrupted by consonants seems, in some magical way, to clarify the composer's musical intentions.

preparation and resolution are treated in an orthodox manner, and the discord itself maintained long enough to assure its audibility, the composer must guard against the tendency of amateur singers to diminish volume on a held note and there should be no hesitation where the sense of the text allows it, in writing the direction "sostenuto" or even "poco crescendo" over the crucial note.

With what degree of flexibility the precepts set forth in this and the preceding chapter may safely be treated, the student will soon discover. Practice and experience will teach him, however, that in the long run it is best to avoid taxing too heavily either the physical capacities or the musicianship of the chorus. There is always more than one way of saying a thing convincingly. High-flown language and verbal preciosity are not the necessary concomitants of eloquence. The meaning of the text at some point may seem to require the employment of extremes of range, of bizarre groupings, or of a type of writing which involves the chorus in the performance of unvocal intervals, unnatural harmonic or contrapuntal progressions or unreasonably dissonant effects. Under these circumstances the student is urged to remember that if he pursues what seems at the moment to be the only possible course, he runs the serious risk of failure; for though he may, perhaps, count on adequate rehearsal, there is the strong possibility that under the stress of performance any one of those many unpredictable psychological upsets to which any chorus is prone may take place. Then, indeed, he will recall that some of the most impressive choral music was written in simple but deeply moving terms; and he will wish with all his heart that he had invited his imagination to play once more over those words which were his undoing.

CHAPTER III

IDIOMATIC CHORAL PRACTICES

THERE ARE certain technical usages not exclusively vocal but particularly valuable in that field, upon which composers have long been wont to rely. These devices constitute a familiar part of every choral singer's experience; he is at home with them in any one of their numerous guises; so that unless they are seriously manhandled by the composer, they may represent a very desirable technical asset. Some of them are more than occasional expedients — they are, rather, principles, and in some types of writing they are almost constants.

THIRDS AND SIXTHS

Writing in thirds and sixths is certainly a principle rather than a device, and its first statement as a musically constructive practice was preceded by what now seems to us a painfully slow evolutionary process. That thirds and sixths were used by untutored singers in the harmonization of their popular songs before ever these intervals were acceptable to musical theory is entirely credible, for they are the very stuff of vocal instinct, and their final accrediting as a reputable artistic means in the form of the *gymel* and *faux bourdon* of the fourteenth and fifteenth centuries doubtless resulted mainly from vocal rather than theoretical considerations. How eagerly composers seized upon these simple formulae as an advance beyond the previously held theory of consonance and dissonance, and how readily musicians accepted the euphony implied in them as the natural substance of music, may be seen in the fact that the use of the

formulae as formulae had, before long, to be limited, and the
principle for which they stood, rather than the practice, became
the recognized procedure. In this there is a lesson for the student, for while thirds and sixths are the very backbone of
choral writing, they soon become cloying and enervating when
unmixed with the sterner material of dissonance.[1] One sees
particularly in English choral music of the sixteenth century
an ideal adaptation of the principle. Example 85 will show how
subtly the method was applied. The formulae themselves do
not appear, but the substance of them (thirds and sixths) is a
pervading presence both melodically and harmonically, sifting
down through the music. In the nineteenth century thirds and

sixths were an integral part of orthodox musical expression.
Thirds, however, perhaps because of their over-exploitation in
the previous century were a relatively incidental use, but sixths,
the outer limits of *faux bourdon,* often in combination with
thirds, offered an unlimited choral resource and they still remain one (Exs. 86, 87, 88, and 89 *).

---

* Copyright in U.S.A. and all countries, 1929, by the Oxford University Press,
London.

[1] How destructive of interest is extended writing in thirds may be learned from
an examination of not a little Italian and English choral music of the eighteenth century. This greatly overworked device was no more than a pretence at simplicity
in an age devoted to formality.

In view of its aggressive euphony, one might doubt the value of such a method to the composer who employs a dissonant medium, but the truth is that in any complex choral texture thirds and sixths offer a secure vocal footing; they are a kind of assured presence, which runs like a binding thread throughout the music however dissonant it may be (Ex. 90*).

* Copyright in U.S.A. and all countries, 1931, by the Oxford University Press, London.

Note that the outer voices upon which the other parts invariably rely are easy to sing by themselves, and may therefore be performed with a degree of confidence which is bound to steady the other and more tonally equivocal parts. Note, further, that the thirds and sixths are constant and lie between the same two voices. For a real understanding of this excerpt (Ex. 91) the

SYMPHONIE DE PSAUMES - 6,7.   Stravinsky.

full score should be consulted. Here thirds and sixths are not persistent nor do they invariably occur between the same voices; out of seventeen chords, however, thirteen contain these intervals. In view of the fact that the accompaniment adds dissonances not found in the vocal score, safeguards beyond the presence of thirds and sixths have been set up. These are a moderate pace in performance and a logical sequential treatment of each voice. Not the least striking feature is the profound knowledge of vocal psychology demonstrated in the technique. (For additional examples of the use of thirds and sixths see also Appendix, Group XVII.)

So versatile is this device that a choral situation in which it is not useful is difficult to imagine. Adeptness in the use of thirds and sixths both as a generality and as a specific method should be acquired by every choral composer. But it cannot be too strongly stated that thirds in any considerable succession between the outer voices should be avoided.

THE WAVE

If you watch the waves at sea you will observe that some appear to be relatively static while others are in motion. One or two rise for an instant to a position of prominence and then give way to others which, in their turn, become the chief figures in an ever-moving pageant. It is, of course, generally the highest wave which draws your glance, but not always; a less conspicuous one may fasten itself on your attention by the beauty of its outline or by its color. If you analyze the whole experience you realize that it has been characterized by a sense of constant change; your eye has been drawn rapidly from place to place, yet you sense not the accidental restlessness of disorder, but only movement arising from a plan that is profoundly logical and that offers infinite variety.

Now the application of all this is pertinent to choral music, because only by change and variety may full advantage be taken of its limited resources. Special effects and passages for women's voices set off against others for men's voices offer legitimate but temporary relief. But the continual overlapping and interplay of the parts, like waves in the contrapuntal tide, each voice displaying at some moment an especial melodic or coloristic significance, that, indeed, is a source of musical strength upon which the composer may draw without fear that it will soon be spent. A sea that is merely choppy does not long stimulate interest; it is the total diversity of motion as well as the shape and color of the separate waves that endlessly projects our imagination forward. Rhythm, therefore, and especially its distribution over the various parts is a conspicuous feature of this method. It is obvious that the most telling "white-caps" will be those that are taken by a leap, and that doubling the crucial voice with another at the same pitch will tend to dilute the full strength of the effect. The reduction of the method to a formula may be seen in Example 92 in which new colors in rapid sequence attract the attention.

Ex. 92.   PSALM 46 - 50.   Schmitt.

In Examples 93 and 94 crosses are inserted to indicate the points at which, because of range, color, or musical or textual significance, a particular part (and occasionally two parts) dominates the situation. (See also Appendix, Group XVIII.)

THE FAN

The Fan Method may be employed in numerous ways and many beautiful examples of it are to be found in both instrumental[2] and choral music. The title is self-explanatory and implies the process of opening or closing the parts, usually the extremes.

[2] See, for instance, the brief introduction to the second theme of the first movement of Schubert's *Unfinished Symphony*.

On the whole this device profits by rare use. It is primarily an *effect,* and it is often most artistic when it is not confined within a measure or two, but is allowed to operate over a larger area, so that the spreading of the voices is more gradual. Here the opening or closing of the fan is normal (Exs. 95 * and 96).

Sometimes one side remains stationary while the other moves. Example 97 is especially interesting as whole chords rather than single voices are involved in the motion. Often both sides will

move in contrary motion while the other segments of the fan either remain stationary or move independently (Exs. 98 and 99), or one side holds firm while the other parts move

* Copyright in U.S.A. and all countries, 1929, by the Oxford University Press, London.

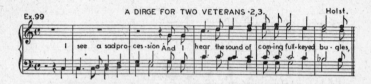

(Ex. 100). Occasionally the fan will open or close in a series of abrupt motions (Ex. 101), or in an alternation of steps and skips (Ex. 102), or the sides will open and close without regard to each other (Exs. 103 and 104; for varied types of the widely used fan process see Appendix, Group XIX).

PIVOTAL NOTES

Pivotal notes are those which remain stationary while the rest of the music is in motion. They are a delight to the singer because they permit him to dwell for a time on his part without complications arising from intervals and words, and they afford him opportunity for a kind of vocal efflorescence which is especially his property. How often, we wonder, does the virtuoso whose privilege it is to blow the swelling note in the overture to *Rienzi* feel himself master of the world to an extent that is possible for the lowly choralist, serenely anchored in the most favorable part of his range, releasing his volume by gentle gradations, and at the final climax, like a bird about to take wing, rising on tiptoe to give his all. Both Brahms and Mendelssohn delighted in creating these moments of vocal exaltation. Brahms, indeed, knew the singer's inmost heart as few composers have, and he frequently did a great service both to his music and to the choristers by sacrificing for the moment the richness of vocal polyphony, and by ascribing to one or another part a melody, obviously solo, but contained within the choral

range. These lines, models of vocality, merit extended study. Take, for example, the opening section of the final chorus of the *Requiem* which begins with a sustained note. This melody is given in turn to the sopranos and basses, and is, in each case, ideally cast.

Not only are pivotal notes vocally grateful, but they may be, too, the one staple factor in a texture which is musically compli-cated. Under such conditions they furnish assurance to the whole chorus. They are a tonal rock in a weary land (Ex. 105).

Characteristic uses of pivotal notes are Examples 106 and 107. Pivotal notes may occur in any number. Here (Ex. 108) four are used simultaneously. (For an example of double pivotal notes which are very common in choral music see Appendix, Group XX.)

Held notes, when carried out to some length, may be considered as pedal points, but these, if really extended, as in the case of No. 3 in the Brahms *Requiem,* belong to instruments which can maintain them indefinitely.[3]

Unless the composer breaks up an impossibly long-sustained note by repeating it to a new word or syllable, he presents the conductor with a problem in breath control which cannot be allowed to go by default. Here are cases of such extended pivotal notes as will require some planning to insure against breath exhaustion before the passage is completed (Exs. 109 and 110). The repeated notes at the end of the Beethoven excerpt are doubtless more by way of increasing the vitality of the passage than of belatedly supplying the singers with a chance to catch their breath. A more humane adjustment will be found in the

[3] Nevertheless, one of the most eloquent and imaginative pedal points of which the author has knowledge is a vocal one; namely, the high soprano note which occurs toward the end of Neptune, the last movement in Holst's suite, *The Planets.* It emerges from the orchestral texture as something disembodied increasing in intensity until it suggests, with an effect that is almost physical, a persistent and a chilling wind.

next examples (Exs. 111 and 112). Only the composer's judgment based upon experience and artistic considerations will tell him whether a long-held note should be broken up, or

whether, as mentioned in Chapter II, p. 39, a line of repeated notes should be absorbed in one note of longer value.

A study of the work of not a few composers will reveal at

least a moderate distrust of the efficacy, in choral music, of repeated notes. It is true, I suppose, that these are not the best choral material in the abstract, but they have proved virtues which cannot be ignored. In the late sixteenth and early seventeenth centuries the ideal of a persistent melodic curve gave way to one that finds a place for whole static areas; groups of repeated notes that are purely declamatory and which render the music alive. They prophesy the dramatic method of text treatment and they are invaluable in making impressive pronouncements of a dignified or significant nature (Exs. 113 and 114; further examples of sustained and repeated notes appear in the Appendix, Group XXI).

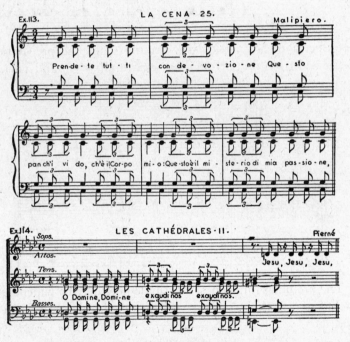

INTRODUCTORY AND CONCLUDING NOTES

Single notes are useful when they serve to introduce a phrase. They may take on the importance of heralds who summon the listener to attention, or they may simply provide one alternative to the customary attack by several parts simultaneously. Examples 115 and 116 present the device in its simplest terms.

Suspensions are particularly striking when the preparation is isolated from the surrounding texture (Exs. 117 and 118).

The preludial function of the single note may be widened to include repeated notes or even whole melodic phrases (Exs. 119 and 120).

Introductory notes are not invariably single (Ex. 121; for various types of introductory notes and phrases see Appendix, Group XXII).

One note or a brief melody given to a single part as the conclusion of a phrase may be most impressive (Exs. 122, 123 and 124; supplementary instances of concluding notes and phrases will be found in Appendix, Group XXIII).

HARMONY AND COUNTERPOINT CONTRASTED

In the fifteenth century the practice of incorporating passages in "familiar style" into polyphonic vocal works was common. All the voices in familiar style, unlike those in harmonic style, preserved a certain amount of melodic independence; but the two are identical in one particular, namely, the homorhythmic movement of the parts. Thus, disregarding all interior differences, both appear as a succession of chords. Familiar style probably originated in the desire of composers to make it possible for the hearer to understand the words which were sung; for in those days it was often the fashion to employ a number of simultaneously sung texts in the course of a single work. Vertical writing, moreover, was capable of offering a salutary contrast to the more active polyphony.[4]

With the establishment of secular music in the sixteenth century and particularly with the rise of opera in the seventeenth, the full value of the chordal method was perceived. Sentiments appropriate to group expression such as are commonly associated with public religious celebrations had found an adequate conveyance through counterpoint. But strong personal feeling or the acute psychological crisis could not be properly articulated through a method that based its appeal on a constant shifting of rhythmic and melodic interest; there was no focal point at which the poignant word or phrase might fall. "Rage," "fear," or "love" when spread through the mazes of counterpoint became emotionally attenuated; but when accompanied by harmony they appeared dynamic, instant, and even dramatic.

In the increasing dependence of counterpoint on harmony it was the former that lost something of its primary character, and the eventual merging of the two styles offered a generally satisfactory medium for choral writing. Though the essentially

---

[4] The use of harmony contrasted with counterpoint was mentioned in Chapter II, p. 50. There it was suggested that one or two harmonically treated verses of a folksong might prepare the way for the greater interest offered in the contrapuntal setting of later verses. Here a briefer, more pointed use of the principle is suggested.

harmonic basis of polyphony was maintained in the eighteenth century, it took that era, and Handel in particular, to revive an appreciation of the fundamental artistic validity of sharp contrast between the harmonic and contrapuntal methods. Again it is impossible to ignore the part which the text plays in all this. The ejaculations "Where? where?" in No. 6 of Brahms's *Requiem,* though not set off by counterpoint, are splendid examples of the percussive effect of the single harmonic stroke. Questions, shouts of exaltation, expressions of confidence, phrases of a meditative character, these, and many other sentiments when harmonically isolated from the surrounding counterpoint furnish the composer with a resource of almost unlimited value (Exs. 125, 126 and 127; see also Appendix, Group XXIV).

Mendelssohn's treatment of this device was particularly

Ex.125. THE MESSIAH - 50. Handel.

happy. In a number of cases he whittles the counterpoint down, so to speak, into a closing passage sometimes strictly harmonic and sometimes melodically harmonic, which is a sort of resolution of all the previous material. By this method he achieves a structural unity and a definiteness of artistic purpose which are characteristic of his unerring sense of formal balance.[5]

THE PARALLEL SWEEP

What is designated as the parallel sweep is not the incidental and inevitable appearance of parallelism in a composition, but

[5] See, for example, the closing passages of the following choruses: "There Shall a Star" (*Christus*), "Happy and Blest are They" (*St. Paul*), "He Watching Over Israel" (*Elijah*).

rather the calculated use of it as an effect comparable in orchestral music to the upsurge of the instruments in the last movement of Tschaikowsky's *Sixth Symphony* (see the full score, 217, Forberg edition). In choral music its presence may often be accounted for by the nature of the text; but even without this warrant it is a device particularly grateful to the choral medium. Sweeps both diatonic and by skip are common, and their vocal effectiveness in many cases is due in no small part to the maintenance, throughout their extent, of a single syllable. Examples 128, 129, and 130 show the diatonic sweep.

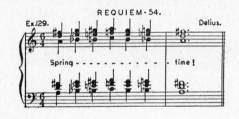

Examples 131 * and 132 are disjunct sweeps.

Sweeps which leap immediately from one limit of the progression to the other are usually of dramatic import (Exs. 133 * and 134).

* Copyright in U.S.A. and all countries, 1929, by the Oxford University Press, London.

Less drastic are those sweeps which are made progressively by means of bringing in single voices or groups of voices as illustrated in the following (Exs. 135 and 136*; for further examples of the sweep see Appendix, Group XXV).

Speech

In comparatively recent times composers have enlarged the boundaries of choral expression by the employment of speech either during the progress of the music or as an interruption to it. Recitation accompanied by music or passages of declamation interspersed throughout the course of a composition are by no means new arrivals especially in the field of dramatic music; but since the adoption of exclusively musical material by types like the oratorio and the cantata, the intrusion of such

* Copyright in U.S.A. and all countries, 1929, by the Oxford University Press, London.

extraneous elements as speech has been rare. Several reasons
may be given for the inclusion of speech in musical performance. First of all there is the prospect of adding an extra-musical
stimulus. The sudden incidence of spoken language in a situation which up to that moment has been exclusively musical
is bound to be exciting. It furnishes too, a relatively violent
contrast in timbres and it is the most trenchant vehicle of
dramatic feeling. Then there is the possibility of supplementing the texture by the element of percussion which is so notably
absent from vocal music. Words that are spoken or shouted
distinctly certainly fall upon the ear with a sharper impact
than is the case when the same words are sung, however
spiritedly. If a somewhat farfetched analogy may be permitted,
one may venture to think that the excitement generated by
violent declamation is akin to that aroused by the tumult of
instruments of percussion. On the other hand, and equally
effective, are such devices as that employed by d'Indy in the
opera *Fervaal*. As Fervaal plays his harp the singers imitate
the twang of the strings by uttering the sound "Ahm" without
reference to any particular pitch. Descriptive touches of this
kind are doubtless valuable and may be carried far into the
sphere of realism, as is the case in Poulenc's *Chanson à boire*
where a conscientious interpretation of the score results in
bibulous outpourings of sound not friendly to gastric insta-
bility. One suspects, however, that a more profound reason than
is suggested by desire for contrast or realism urges the composer now and then to vary music by speech; namely, the feeling that certain passages of prose or poetry do not readily
submit to musical treatment, or that others, because they are,
as literature, self-sufficient, lose something of their significance
when accompanied by music. Take, for example, the following
passage from Carter's *Defense of Corinth*:

> Some from the fields brought into the fortified places their moveables, cat-
> tle, corn, wine, fruit, victuals and other necessary provisions. Others did
> fortify and rampire their walls, set up little fortresses, bastions, squared
> ravelins, digged trenches, cleansed countermines, fenced themselves with

gabions, contrived platforms, emptied casemates, erected the cavalliers, mortaised barbacans, etc.[6]

Any composer, however resourceful, would be hard put to it to find music for such a passage, and Carter justifiably leaves it to be spoken.[7]

The application of speech as an offset to choral singing is susceptible of much variety. It may call for the single speaker, as in Stravinsky's *Oedipus Rex,* Honegger's *King David,* or Caplet's *Miroir de Jésus,* or it may require participation by the chorus as in the instances cited earlier or as in Holst's *Hymn of*

[6] The text, with which the composer has freely dealt, may be found on p. 50 of volume II of Rabelais, *Five Books of the Lives, Heroic Deeds and Sayings of Gargantua and his son Pantagruel,* translated by Urquhart and Motteux (London: A. H. Bullen, 1904).

[7] In view of the increasing use of group speech in choral composition, it is interesting to note that the principle has become crystallized in a form which Professor Robert Sanders of the Music Department of the University of Indiana calls "concerted speech" and which he describes as "something almost, but not quite, verging on chanting."

Details of this method, now included in the curriculum of some institutions of learning, may be discovered by consulting C. de Banke, *The Art of Choral Speech* (Boston: W. H. Baker Co., 1937).

Not long ago the author was privileged to examine Professor Sanders' setting for chorus and orchestra of Walt Whitman's *Mystic Trumpeter* in which concerted speech plays a not inconsiderable rôle. The occasion seemed propitious for learning at first hand a composer's attitude towards this device and his reasons for selecting it in these particular circumstances. "I was convinced," writes Professor Sanders in reply to the author's queries, "of the great theatrical effectiveness and power of expression in concerted speech whenever the text was great enough to stand on its own feet. Perhaps as a matter of individual temperament, I have often felt frustration when faced with the task of setting words to music. In a rough way I have noticed gradations in this sense of frustration. It appears greatest when the proposed text is most concentrated, most meaningful, most complete in itself, and the sense of frustration is least when the proposed text is in a foreign language, more particularly when it is a static language such as Latin, a language remote from every-day usage.

"For some reason this sense of frustration did not bother me during the whole period when I contemplated and executed *The Mystic Trumpeter* except for one section whose consideration did trouble me. That was the section dealing with war. I came more and more to have a conviction that anything musical I might append to Whitman's words would weaken and dissipate the effective expression of the grim horror which this section of his poem seeks to convey. I came finally to feel that logically there were only two things that could be done with it: 1. To set it musically in so extraordinary, so compelling, so unprecedentedly dramatic a manner that the music would succeed in heightening, not lessening, the expression. 2. To do as little as possible to it, to do little more than chant it.

"Then recollecting a choral speech performance I had heard, I realized that here was the medium I was seeking."

Jesus and Stravinsky's *Les Noces*. There are certainly two opinions as to the aesthetic validity of mixing choral singing with the spoken word. In a sense, it revives the old antagonism between French and Italian opera. Whether, in the long run, it will prove a rewarding device, no one can now foresee.

CHAPTER IV

POLYVOCAL WRITING

THE SOPRANO, alto, tenor, and bass cover, among them, the total vocal range, and practical considerations such as the size of the average chorus and the individual competence of the typical choral singer may seem to make it unwise to exceed these traditional four parts. Theoretically, however, the composer may weave as many strands as he wishes within the vocal compass. Because four have been generally adopted, we term choral music employing parts in excess of that number *polyvocal*.

Although every period — including our own — since the establishment of music as an art has produced notable examples of polyvocal writing, it is the sixteenth century in particular that is outstanding. Counterpoint was then the native musical language of the choral composer, and it ran copiously and uninhibited. The unlabored perfection of the polyvocal style of that time must persuade us that the problem presented by the composition of a motet in forty voices was a spatial and not a technical one. The composer with only artistic considerations in mind adopted the number which best suited his purpose. Lassus' two-part vocal canons are identical with his polyvocal works in the effortless quality of their technique; and the same is true of the three-part sacred and secular writing of the composers of the Golden Age, as is evident when one contrasts their work in those simpler forms with their many-voiced madrigals and motets.

The cultivation of the polyvocal style [1] was markedly slighter

[1] The term "polyvocal" is generally used throughout this chapter to indicate that type of writing which involves the manipulation of more than four voices treated as a unit; i.e. not subdivided into two or more choruses, a style which is called "polychoral" or "polychoric."

in the periods which followed, and for this many reasons, properly belonging to a history of choral music, might be suggested. But for the student the all important fact to be noted is that regardless of the period, whether sixteenth or nineteenth century, and independent of the style, whether modal or tonal, every successful writer of polyvocal music has been a contrapuntist of distinction. No one is justified in entering this field of composition unless his mastery of the complexities of choral style and of counterpoint which is a basic factor in it is so complete that his work will be quite free of any suspicion of calculated labor.

Which parts the composer chooses will depend largely on the character of the text and on the choral color desired. In the sixteenth century voices were selected according to categories which might be described as "high," "middle," and "low." [2] Concentration was, apparently, on the general area to be covered by a given voice rather than on any particular vocal timbre. For example, Giovanni Gabrieli's famous motet *Angelus ad pastores,* which is really a double chorus of six parts each, is scored as follows: Cantus, Septima pars, Altus, Octava pars, Quintus, Sextus, Duodecima pars, Undecima pars, Nona pars, Tenor, Bassus I, and Bassus II. In assigning any one of these parts to a modern singer, it is necessary, of course, to determine first which one of our four traditional voices will best accommodate itself to the range. Even so, after following through the greater part of one voice and having decided that it is suitable, say, to the alto compass, a few notes may be discovered which are definitely in the tenor range.[3]

In spite of the apparently opulent scoring of the polyvocal music of the sixteenth century, one lesson may certainly be learned from it — namely, that of economy of range. The *tessitura* of an entire polychoral piece, often a fairly long one,

[2] These designations are used by the contemporary composer Percy Grainger in his choral music in preference to soprano, alto, etc.

[3] Present day conductors of sixteenth-century polyvocal music are frequently forced to divert singers from one part to supply certain notes of another.

is likely to be surprisingly restricted. Sometimes the lowest note which at any time occurs in the bass part, and the highest one in the soprano, represent a distance of not more than two and one half octaves. Furthermore, the range of any one voice may be so small — perhaps no larger than a ninth — that it might be performed by either of two adjacent parts. Indeed, the expansiveness of Monteverdi in this particular appears lavish when compared with that of his immediate predecessors. But most remarkable is the retention of a voice for a long period within a very limited compass. Occasionally one part will have as many as thirty notes within the range of a fifth.[4] Yet monotony is never a reproach in spite of an apparent defiance of our modern conception of the technical means of bringing about variety in this style of composition. It is a commonplace in the technique of the period to write page after page of fascinating multi-vocal music in which individual voices as well as the total range are strictly confined. In the first place, except where familiar style is used, marked rhythmic differentials among the parts are generally present. Inherent in this is the plentiful use of rests. Parts are withdrawn at intervals, altering not only the body but also the color of the texture. This is of the first importance owing to the uniformity of choral color. In the orchestra, a single voice may remain dominant for some time because of the individuality of its timbre; but a single vocal part easily becomes merged with the general tone and may only be effective when intermittently employed.[5] And finally, neighboring voices are forever crossing each other to produce varying degrees of light and shade. All this, of course, is applicable, as method, to ordinary four part writing; but with vocal resources which permit groupings of four sopranos or four basses with all the intermediate shades of color made possible by manifold

---

[4] For examples of restraint in the matter of range see Ferrarese, *Ave et Gaude;* Zarlino, *Nigra Sum;* and Ingegneri, *Dolorosi martir.*

[5] For one reason or another composers have sometimes preferred to set up one uniform and unusual color which maintains throughout a movement. Thus Berlioz and Chabrier sometimes omit the alto voice entirely.

combinations of the voices, the choral composer will find a stronger challenge to his resourcefulness than is offered by the four part medium.[6]

Example 137 is typical of one aspect of sixteenth-century polyvocal style. The harmony is comparatively static so that the chief interest lies in the treatment of the entrances, in the rhythmic diversity and in the various colors attained by using the different ranges of a single voice. Where there is less animation in the parts, the harmony may change more frequently.

Because the sources of polyvocal technique are to be sought in the sixteenth century, almost all that has been said thus far applies particularly to the music of that period; and although later practice is certainly founded on sixteenth-century method, certain details should be noted which affect this style con-

Ex. 137.   AL MORMORAR · 93.   Gastoldi.

[6] An interesting specimen of multivocal scoring is Robert Carver's motet for nineteen voices, *O bone Iesu*, which calls for the following parts: 4S — 3A — 9T — 3B.

spicuously in the eighteenth century and afterwards. These result in great part from the expansion of both the harmonic vocabulary and the vocal range; from counterpoint more harmonically controlled; and from the much greater use of an accompaniment. Noticeable, also, even as early as the seventeenth century, is a tendency to sacrifice pure vocality in the interests of a modified keyboard style.[7]

Bach's *Magnificat* may be taken as an example of the late Thorough-bass period product in polyvocal style; albeit the work itself is crowned with Bach's own genius. The accompaniment supplies an added color resource and contributes richness to the whole texture at the same time that it permits thickening or thinning of either participant without loss of

[7] Examples of this tendency may be plainly observed in Lotti's two settings of the *Crucifixus*, one in eight and one in ten parts, and in Frescobaldi's *Sei Madrigali a cinque voci*.

harmonic stability. From the point of view of variety, this is often desirable as it allows the use of a solo voice, or of two contrapuntal parts unsupported by a vocal harmonic foundation; a principle well exemplified in the few measures that follow the opening chords of the Gloria in Bach's *Magnificat*.

Nineteenth- and twentieth-century polyvocal technique pays full tribute to the skill of the sixteenth century, but there are two features which are particularly characteristic of the later style: the voice grouping, which has adopted something from orchestral practice,[8] and the emphasis on one part as the chief melody. The music of Russian choral composers like Tschaikowsky, Gretchaninoff, Kastalsky, and Tschesnokoff is particularly notable in respect to grouping in harmonic style; the wide range between basses and sopranos affording an opportunity for effects that are distinctly suggestive of the orchestra.

Among the most common scorings in polyvocal writing[9] are the following:

Five Voices	Six Voices	Seven Voices	Eight Voices
a. S–A–2T–B	a. S–2A–T–2B [10]	a. S–2A–2T–2B	a. 2S–2A–2T–2B
b. 2S–2A–T	b. 2S–A–2T–B	b. 2S–2A–2T–B	b. S–2A–2T–3B
c. 2S–A–T–B	c. 2S–A–T–2B		c. 3S–2A–2T–B
d. S–A–T–2B	d. 2S–3A–T		
e. 2S–2T–B	e. 3S–A–T–B		

Of the four polyvocal groupings listed above, by far the most common is the five-part arrangement *SSATB,* with the two sopranos of identical range and comparable in their function

[8] The use of parallel octaves — not unknown in the sixteenth century — is very common in polyvocal style where it resembles the orchestral method of writing a melodic line in two or three strata.

[9] Polyvocal style is so common that the student will not fail to find many examples of it. For reasons which study will make apparent the following pieces may be considered valuable as models:

Tomkins, *When David Heard;* Sweelinck, *Born Today;* Handel, "Lift Up Your Heads" (*Messiah*); Parry, *There is an Old Belief;* Greene, *How Long Wilt Thou Forget Me;* Pizzetti, *La Rondine;* Gretchaninoff, *The Echo;* Vaughan Williams, *Serenade to Music* (written for 16 solo voices); Mozart, *Great Mass in C minor;* Handel, *Dettingen Te Deum;* Bach, *B minor Mass;* Mendelssohn, *St. Paul;* Berlioz, *The Damnation of Faust;* Brahms, *Gesang der Parzen;* Fauré, *The Birth of Venus;* Dvořák, *Stabat Mater;* Stravinsky, *Les Noces;* d'Indy, *Le Chant de la Cloche.*

In the editions listed on p. 104, footnote 17, will be found much polyvocal as well as polychoral material. For added examples of the former see Appendix, Group XXVI.

[10] Brahms was much given to this arrangement.

to the first and second violins of the orchestra. The possibility of brightening the texture by the employment of two upper parts instead of one, and the opportunities for contrapuntal expansion in a range in which every device of counterpoint may be made effective, did not fail to appeal to a multitude of composers from the sixteenth century to the end of the Thorough-bass period. During that time the *SSATB* scoring is almost as often used as the traditional *SATB* arrangement.

By the term "polychoral" is meant the grouping of the voices in a polyvocal work into two or more choruses. Whether or not a work should be classified as polyvocal or polychoral is sometimes difficult to decide, because elements of both may be present.[11] Moreover, if an editor feels that the nature of the piece calls for an arbitrary sub-division of the parts into choruses, he may make that modification. The essence of polychoral style is antiphony. Regardless of the actual physical separation of the choirs one from another — and polychoral music is most effective when this condition is present — it is assumed that in polychoral style each chorus will maintain an individual life of its own. This means that although all or parts of the different choirs often sing together, in many instances one choir will make its entries and departures as a unit, and for periods of varying length it will be silent. Furthermore, the "dialogue" and "echo" principles will frequently be invoked.[12]

What has just been referred to as the dialogue or echo effect is particularly useful as a dramatic means and also as a color device, provided the contrasting timbres in the opposing groups are wisely selected. It is evident, however, that the mere setting against each other of two identical choral forces in block formation was in earlier periods often deemed sufficient. This

[11] Marco da Gagliano's *Su l'Africane Arene* is a mixture of polyvocal and polychoral styles.

[12] Clearly identifiable as belonging to the dialogue type are: Montella, *Filiae Jerusalem;* Trabacci, *Venite;* A. Gabrieli, *Dialogo;* Durante, *Misericordias Domini.* In Lassus' *O La, O Che Buon Êco* two choruses answer each other exactly, and when one of the choruses is placed off-stage the effect of a perfect echo may be obtained. For an interesting example of a revival of the seventeenth-century dialogue, or better, conversational technique as it is found, for example, in Hammerschmidt and Pelham Humphrey, see the final chorus of Haydn's *The Seasons.*

principle of opposition applies equally to polyvocal style wherein, because it is primarily contrapuntal, the virtue of color contrast may be supplemented by rhythmic interest. In spite of all that has been said about the color element in sixteenth-century polyvocal music, one suspects that the composers of that time were more concerned with this rhythmic matter than with setting up a varied color scheme; for when echo-like or responsive passages occur, the same set of voices was often used for successive statements of the material in sequence. Thus the color element, in our modern sense, seems to play a surprisingly small part in the calculation. Example 138 is interesting because it embodies both rhythm and color; the latter represented by the comparatively brief appearance, not of patches of choral color, but of individual timbres. Ex-

Ex.138. DONNA, SE M'ANCIDETE-17 Gesualdo.

ample 138 gains not a little of its effect from the impact of the consonants *ch* and *t*. These seem to project each new color with a particular degree of clarity and to heighten measurably the rhythmic excitement. A most ingenious employment of this principle of percussive consonants is to be found in Chorus VI of Randall Thompson's *The Peaceable Kingdom* (Ex. 139).

Just as Palestrina's exalted style stands without a rival in its field, so the finest models of polychoral writing are to be sought in the works of the sixteenth-century Venetian School. St. Mark's was the center of this movement, and in the capacity for extracting from the polychoric medium all that is imagi-

Ex.139. THE PEACEABLE KINGDOM · 65. Randall Thompson.

nable in variety and effectiveness, the supremacy of the Venetians has rarely been challenged. In a long line of outstanding musicians who served at St. Mark's, Giovanni Gabrieli is generally counted as the chief figure. His music is not only distinguished in its own right, but is, as well, a prophet of tendencies which were to be increasingly influential after his time. There is the evidence of a strong reaction against the older type of vocal polyphony shown by the presence of definite pulses, of a clearcut harmonic framework for the counterpoint, and of an unmistakable dramatic quality in the musical speech. The adoption of certain features of instrumental style previously mentioned in this chapter is manifest not only in the types of melodic figuration but also in a kind of exuberant virtuosity which suggests the same composer's organ works and concerted canzoni.[13] The choral writing by itself is sonorous to a degree, and when the Venetian custom of supplementing the voices

[13] Gabrieli occasionally used the polychoral method for purely instrumental music, dividing the instruments into two or three groups.

by a brass choir was invoked the effect must have been overwhelming.

Example 140, drawn from Giovanni Gabrieli's *Jubilate Deo*, is characteristic of the tense brilliance of the Venetian style.

Other works of Gabrieli which merit study are *In Ecclesiis* with its brilliant instrumental accompaniment, and, of a different character, *O Jesu mi dulcissime* and the triple chorus *Benedictus*. A study of polychoral style in general will prove that the wisest composers have been sparing rather than ex-

travagant in their use of extensive rhythmic resource, especially where the music is borne by two and especially three
choruses simultaneously. Under these conditions the rhythm
generally tends towards simplification.[14]

It was the nineteenth century that delighted in multiplying
the resources of polyvocal style. The preceding era, to be sure,
had a flair for a kind of exhibitionism which led to the inclusion in the performance of all sorts of elements. Oratorios had
their comic interludes, *Te Deums* were interlarded with minu-
ets, there were off-stage orchestras, invisible choirs, and fire-
works and cannon. The post-romantic fervor for lavish means
produced not a little over-stuffed musical furniture; bloated
works which call into action a veritable army of performers
both vocal and instrumental. The mere numerical aspect of
such an array with the resulting volume is, in itself, undeniably
impressive; and one would hardly say that Schönberg's *Gur-
relieder* or Mahler's *Eighth Symphony* would be less effective
if their composers had not blown them up to such colossal
proportions. Yet a study of such scores prompts speculation
as to whether the ideas embodied in the music could not have
been as forcibly expressed by less sumptuous means. These are
matters of individual judgment and it would be futile to en-
large on them. The prototype of all this expansiveness is, of
course, Berlioz' gargantuan *Requiem*. That work is, in the
main, effective; but Berlioz' successors were not always equally
convincing.

The following scorings within the polychoral scheme are
typical:

Double Chorus

a.	(Cho. 1) S–A–T–B (Cho. 2) S–A–T–B	c.	(Cho. 1) S–A–2T (Cho. 2) S–A–T–B	e.	(Cho. 1) 2S–A–B (Cho. 2) S–A–T–B
b.	(Cho. 1) 2S–2A (Cho. 2) 2T–2B	d.	(Cho. 1) 2S–T–B (Cho. 2) 2S–T–B	f.	(Cho. 1) S–A–2T (Cho. 2) S–A–2T

[14] There may have been a practical reason for this in the music written for St.
Mark's. All conductors are aware of the difficulty of preserving unity when choirs are
posted at some distance from one another.

Triple Chorus [15]

	(Cho. 1) S–A–T–B		(Cho. 1) 2S–2A
a.	(Cho. 2) S–A–T–B	c.	(Cho. 2) 2T–2B
	(Cho. 3) S–A–T–B		(Cho. 3) 2T–2B
	(Cho. 1) S–A–T–B		(Cho. 1) 2S–A–T
b.	(Cho. 2) S–A–T–B	d.	(Cho. 2) S–A–T–B
	(Cho. 3) 2T–2B		(Cho. 3) 1T–3B

It will be seen that four voices normally make up each unit within the polychoral group, but that number is not invariable. A single part may occasionally be written *divisi* for a few measures, or the composer may choose to employ more than four voices as Vecchi sometimes did. The number of voices may be suggested by the words, as in Paine's *The Nativity* set to Milton's text, where at one point nine-part writing is appropriately used.[16] No subtle differentiations, however, seem to be implied in Vecchi's case as he uses a double five-part chorus for pieces of such opposed character as the *Beati Omnes* and *Trinklied*.[17]

[15] The polychoral scheme rarely includes more than three choruses. Schütz wrote what may be called quadruple choruses, though the probability of instrumental participation in these makes analysis difficult.

[16] And with your ninefold harmony
Make up full consort to the angelic symphony.
Milton — *On the Morning of Christ's Nativity*

[17] Especially worthy of study are the following:
Carissimi, *Kyrie;* Handel, "And the Children of Israel sigh'd" (*Israel in Egypt*); S. Wesley, *In Exitu Israel;* Mozart, "Osanna in Excelsis" and "Qui Tollis" (*Great Mass in C minor*); Schütz, *Sing to the Lord a New Song;* Taneyef, *From Land to Land;* Vaughan Williams, *Mass in G Minor, Sancta Civitas;* Randall Thompson, *The Peaceable Kingdom;* Pizzetti, *Requiem Mass;* Delius, *Requiem;* Walton, *Belshazzar's Feast;* K. Thomas, *Passionsmusik*.

Most of the pieces in the foregoing list were written after the heyday of polyvocal style. A number of sixteenth- and seventeenth-century works in this field have been published in modern editions, but the vast literature is available mainly in monumental collections like the following:

L'Arte musicale in Italia, Instituzioni e Monumenti dell' arte musicale Italiana, Musica Sacra (Peters I), *Sammlung vorzügliche Gesangstücke, Musica Divina* (Commer), *Musica Divina* (Proske), *The English Madrigal School, Tudor Church Music, Denkmäler deutscher Tonkunst, Denkmäler der Tonkunst in Österreich, Denkmäler der Tonkunst in Bayern, Hispaniae Schola Musica Sacra, Das Chorwerk;* Schütz, *Sämmtliche Werke;* Purcell, *The Works of Henry Purcell;* Monteverdi, *Tutti le opere.* Added examples of polychoral style are given in Appendix, Group XXVII.

The diversity of technique in polyvocal and polychoral writing is so wide that the author prefers not to increase the roster of separate works, a procedure which might be taken to imply the need for only a limited examination of an extremely complex technique.

One idiomatic use of polychoral writing peculiar to the nineteenth and twentieth centuries, and one which has added immeasurably to the effectiveness of that style, is the employment of the principle of "perspective." This involves the use of chorus and semi-chorus, or chorus and solo quartet, so that instead of the coöperation of two or three relatively equal bodies of singers there is a tonal foreground and background.[18]

Contrast is, of course, a basic factor in this practice; from this point of view, to be sure, "perspective" has long been a feature of choral and instrumental music. It may be observed in the alternating use of a solo group and a full chorus in the seventeenth-century English verse anthem, and in the *concertino* and *ripieno* of the eighteenth-century concerto grosso. Its modern use, however, implies something more. The interpretation may be entirely subjective; but there seems to be a less well-defined opposition of one group to another; a subtly calculated use of such details as color and *tessitura* contribute an element that is almost visual. A particularly imaginative use of the idea of musical perspective is to be found in Willan's *An Aprostrophe to the Heavenly Host*. Example 141 is a quadruple chorus in which the resources of both perspective and color are ingeniously arrayed.

Before employing either the polyvocal or the polychoral method the composer should ask himself whether the ends of eloquence will not be as well served by a less involved procedure. A polyvocal score, it is true, is an impressive sight. It implies full mastery of choral technique and it suggests that the musical ideas are somehow more profound, more expansive, than those which find adequate fulfilment in the commonplace four-part "anthem" score. It should be remembered,

[18] The coloristic possibilities of this scheme are manifold as will be observed in the following works: Liszt, *Missa Solemnis;* Holst, *The Hymn of Jesus;* Vaughan Williams, *G minor Mass;* and the Verdi *Requiem.*

The instrumental application of this idea may be seen in Vaughan Williams' *Fantasia on a Theme of Thomas Tallis* for triple string orchestra. The third and smallest group is often placed at the back of the stage so that the effect in sound corresponds to the aspect of a picture in which three groups of figures are arranged at varying distances from the eye.

Ex.141. AN APOSTROPHE TO THE HEAVENLY HOSTS - 17. Willan.

however, that some of the noblest music has been confined to a single line, to two lines and to three. One dislikes to think of how much music paper has been wasted and of how many irritating practical obstacles have been set up for conductors by those whose ambitions outran their better judgment in this matter of polyvocal writing. Three risks attend any excursion into the polyvocal or polychoral field: first, the weakening of the lines, since the division of any part, such as the soprano, into two sections means that the volume of each line will be less than it would be if the whole part were united; second, the possibility of needless duplication, as polyvocal style is only fully effective when each voice has a reason for being; in the same way, polychoral style justifies itself only when a single chorus is not adequate; and third, overthickening of the texture in a medium in which clarity and richness are provedly obtainable in plain four-part writing.

If, then, the composer is persuaded that contrapuntal complexity, an unusually substantial tonal fabric, or a wide diversity of color is essential, then polyvocal style is his obvious resource. Again, should the situation either musical or textual call for antiphony or the employment of the perspective device, a polychoral setting may properly be undertaken. In either case, the reasons must be valid and the technique sure; otherwise artificiality and ineptitude will be the harvest.

CHAPTER V

ACCOMPANIMENT

THE WORD "accompaniment" is an old-fashioned term used to describe the subordinate rôle played by one or more participants in a composition. The contributions of the orchestra of pre-Verdian Italian opera, in general, fulfil this definition. They were often no more than harmony broken up into the familiar rhythmic rum-tum formula so aptly parodied by Sullivan in his operettas. Accompaniments they assuredly were, for they did little more than walk servilely beside the royal vocal presence. But instruments, and the orchestra in particular, now offer so much by way of interest and variety that composers have accorded them an increasingly important place.

The lines of demarcation between types of choral accompaniment are as fluid as those which separate the various choral groupings, and to attempt to catalogue them according to their technical substance would be an endless task and one without great value. The most effective method, perhaps, is to classify accompaniments on the basis of their relation to the choral part. Thus there seem to be four main orders. No one of these will probably persist for long, and in a single composition several of them may be found. Classification of this sort, being in the main subjective, leaves ample room for disagreement, particularly in the case of types three and four. A simple illustration of the first type, which might be termed "skeleton" or "reduction" appears in Example 142.

Rarely do composers now think it necessary to reinforce the chorus for any length of time with a literal copy of the notes it is asked to sing. Often, to be sure, a strict reduction is intended only as an aid in practice; in which case it is marked "For

rehearsal only." Occasionally, as a contrast to a more florid type of accompaniment, or as support to a section the importance of which is primarily choral, though too long to be left unaccompanied, or in a passage of marked vocal difficulty where the composer dares not risk any instrumental distraction, he will simply duplicate the voice parts in the accompaniment with perhaps a lower octave added in the bass. But generally the composer sees to it that while the notes of the voice parts are somewhere present in the accompaniment, his prudence is made less obvious by the assignment to the orchestra, let us say, of independent material.[1]

Example 143 displays the second or "background" type, a reduction broken up into figures which serve not only as a

[1] The two examples in Appendix, Group XXVIII, illustrate this procedure. In the Honegger excerpt the difficulty of vocal intonation is offset by supporting the voices with oboes, bassoons, and horn. At the same time, however, the strings, clarinets, and flutes pursue their own devices (see the full score, pp. 210, 211). In the Brahms excerpt the difficulty is a rhythmic one. There the chorus is aided in its attacks by first violins, violas, double basses, flutes, oboes, clarinets, bassoons, and tympani. The figuration is carried on by the second violins and cellos (see full score, pp. 21, 22). In neither case does the vocal score indicate the full measure of orchestral reinforcement.

support but which also contribute something by way of rhythmic animation. The use of non-harmonic notes is not foreign to the idea of such an accompaniment. In this connection ostinato basses are valuable, and even arpeggios may take on a semblance of contrapuntal interest. This kind of accompaniment, like type one, is usually employed where the choral material is so interesting and so signficant that the composer wishes to set up no more than an unobtrusive background of only nominal musical importance.

The third type may be termed "partially independent." These are accompaniments which claim a certain amount of interest in their own right but which do not possess sufficient individuality apart from the choral material to entitle them to be considered as compositions by themselves (Ex. 144).

The fourth and last type might be classified as "independent." Accompaniments of this order are of two kinds: first, those which could stand alone as music separated from the vocal part, yet which do not over-top the chorus in the interest of the listener. Such accompaniments serve, in the main, as coöperative artistic personalities sharing the interest of the chorus (Ex. 145). In the second division of type four, the main significance of the musical idea is to be sought in the instrumental part, as is illustrated by Example 146.[2]

Instrumental preludes, postludes, and interludes, though a powerful means of adding interest and variety, should never be introduced without reason. The use of interludes, particu-

[2] A feature common to both classifications of type four is the reduction in the number of choral parts.

larly as regards their number and length, requires the exercise of the most careful judgment. It is assumed that in most cases the thought which abides in the words will be continuously unfolded by the singers; frequent instrumental interruption, therefore, is a distraction from the main issue. Obviously there will be places in the text which offer normal occasion for affording the chorus a chance to rest; and there will be places where, for a time, instruments alone will appear to be the appropriate resource. Sometimes the chorus will present an idea which the accompaniment will expand in a characteristically instrumental fashion; or the accompaniment will comment on what the chorus is about to sing. Brahms was a master hand at integrating choral and instrumental material, and the *Requiem* is literally a treatise on this subject. The expansion of the idea of the first chorus, for example, is continuous in spite of frequent changes of medium, and the melody of the instrumental prelude to No. 4 prophecies the entrance of the chorus by

appearing as an inversion of the vocal melody of the first phrase.

Under certain circumstances, however, the composer may elect to set the chorus and accompaniment in opposition, either in dialogue form or, in extreme cases, generally of a dramatic nature, as something in the style of an argument (Ex. 147). Wastefulness in the treatment of the bass part is a sure sign of the cramped contrapuntal hand. Vocal sonority is no match

for that of instruments, and to double the choral and instrumental basses often results in a total loss of effectiveness insofar
as the singing basses are concerned.[3] The presence of an additional part, moreover, contributes considerably to the resources of the contrapuntist. An examination of Bach's choruses,
to cite the work of but one composer, will show the virtue of
capitalizing on the presence of two basses. It would seem worth
while to quote one brief and subtle instance of differentiation
between the functions of the choral and instrumental basses
(Ex. 148). The crucial note in this passage is the *D* flat in the
orchestra at the beginning of the second measure. To have
doubled it in the instruments and voices would have rendered
the choral bass part of no effect; whereas, by remaining on

[3] The futility of such doubling is especially marked in the case of a pedal point.

E flat the singers preserve their individuality and strengthen the choral texture.

With the establishment of instrumental style the accompaniment became a fairly steady feature of choral composition; at the same time there was apparently little appreciation of the variety to be obtained by introducing unaccompanied sections in the course of a single work. In general, music was either accompanied or *a cappella* throughout. The eighteenth century occasionally found use for the brief unaccompanied choral section and employed it with striking effect. Even now, after many hearings, the omission of instruments at the words "Let there be light" in Haydn's *Creation,* with the overwhelming orchestral entrance on the word "light," never fails in impressiveness. Concentration on the development of every avenue of musical interest led, in the nineteenth century, to the frequent and not always successful exploitation of the idea of alternating accompanied and unaccompanied passages. When this method is invoked great care must be taken not to involve the chorus in difficulties of intonation. Failure to observe this warning is almost certain to result in embarrassment; for the chorus will, in many cases, have lost its pitch, and the eventual entrance of instruments will serve painfully to emphasize that fault. Nor, for the same reason, should the *a cappella* sections be very long.[4] Occasional pitch cues, inserted in the midst of

[4] The chorus "Quaerens me" in Berlioz' *Requiem* is a perennial stumbling block to singers. It is of such length that few choral organizations find themselves in agreement with the orchestra when it finally enters at the beginning of the "Lacrymosa."

the unaccompanied section, are no more than a gesture, for once a chorus has started to flat more than incidental instrumental prompting is necessary to restore tonal propriety.[5] Provided the composer's scheme requires that an extended *a cappella* passage be followed immediately by the accompaniment, there is but one safe method to employ, and that is to introduce the instruments in a key so distant from that in which the unaccompanied section closed that the disparity will automatically negative any suggestion of a tonal catastrophe.[6]

There is an all too familiar type of accompaniment which is obviously superimposed on the choral substance. The voices have been written first and then the instrumental part has been added. Such a practice is not to be commended. An accompanied choral work should represent a single idea whose manifestations, both choral and instrumental, grow up simultaneously. It makes no difference what particular method the composer chooses to achieve this ideal, provided the result justifies the means. Indeed, the writing of an accompaniment should never be a mechanical or a routine matter. The first question a composer should ask himself is as to whether an accompaniment is desirable; for if it exists merely as vocal support it may well have small reason for being. Its nature should, in the end, be dictated much less by practical considerations than by what the text suggests and by the requirements of an integrated work of art.

KEYBOARD ACCOMPANIMENTS

It is safe to say that most choral composers possess some facility on the pianoforte. This is at once an advantage and a disadvantage, for while it permits writing in a style that is effective, it often results in an over-demand on the capabilities of the accompanist. The bad or even inadequate performance of an accompaniment may quite ruin the effect of a choral

---

[5] For an example of a half-hearted reminder to the chorus of its responsibility for preserving the pitch see the "Pie Jesu" in Cherubini's *Requiem in D minor* for men's voices.

[6] For a skilful solution according to this formula, see the closing pages of Vaughan Williams' *Lord, thou hast been our refuge.*

work. Choruses do not, in general, command the services of really expert pianists, and the composer is well-advised when he writes an accompaniment that is within the capabilities of the *proficient* rather than the *virtuoso* pianist.

An important consideration is the balance of sonority and of color between the voices and accompaniment. The long-continued occupation by both of a single sector of the range, especially when there is mere duplication of the vocal and instrumental parts, results in a kind of artistic stalemate in which neither participant in the project appears at his best. Too many thirds, in particular, result in a thickness which is disturbing, especially where the third is in a middle or lower register. In such cases the omission of the third from either the instrumental or the vocal part is often advisable. The very fact that the chorus persistently and efficiently holds the middle ground leaves the accompaniment free to exploit from time to time the Beethovian method of separating the hands at some distance from one another. In general, the most satisfactory type of pianoforte accompaniment is that which avails itself of the full compass of the instrument, and which takes advantage of devices that are characteristically pianistic. Rhythmic figures which stand out against a choral background are especially valuable. The sustaining and the damper pedals, furthermore, are sources of interesting color variety. There are, as well, pulsatile effects, runs, trills, arpeggii, glissandi, and other means which may legitimately be employed in building up a coöperative and stimulating partnership.

A word should be said in behalf of the four-hand accompaniment, which, for practical reasons, is too seldom resorted to. It is true that the cost of printing an extra two lines on every page may force the publisher to put a price on the music higher than that customarily asked. It is also true that most choruses have but one accompanist, and these difficulties composers must, of course, take into account. One doubts, on the other hand, whether there are many who would allow such deterrents to override artistic considerations. The truth is that the resources of the pianoforte accompaniment are practically doubled by the use of two players, and if the second part is judiciously written there are not many choruses which cannot supply someone from their ranks capable of performing it. The four-hand accompaniment is the obvious solution to the problem of arranging orchestral accompaniments for the pianoforte.[7] Indeed if one compares many two-hand versions of orchestral works with their originals he is too often shocked to discover how much has been sacrificed to necessity; furthermore, to make a four-hand accompaniment from one arranged for two hands is again to risk the omission of much that is vital.[8]

Of all forms of accompaniment, that for organ is the most cavalierly dealt with. In most cases an organist is asked to play a score conceived in terms of the pianoforte, and if the accompaniment in question happens to be a reduction of orchestral writing, the task is either an impossible one, or else it demands superlative powers both as performer and arranger. Few organists, even if they are competent to do so, take the trouble to write out a separate part based on the pianoforte version of the orchestral accompaniment of a chorus by Bach or Handel; and so, if called upon to play such works at service, they either proclaim the score not adaptable to the organ (in which

[7] Arrangements and transcriptions of any kind represent compromise and a distortion of the composer's primary intent. The self-respecting musician deplores them while at the same time he respects, within certain limits, their value. Taste and consideration for the rights of the composer will decide whether an arrangement is warranted, and if so, whether it has been equitably and skilfully dealt with. The justification, if any, for this practice may occur in the case of a work which, owing to the nature or extent of its resources, might be seldom heard in its original form. Educational policy, too, may be invoked to bring music within the performing range of school or college groups which would otherwise be committed to a limited experience. Regarding arrangements, two admonitions may be earnestly laid down: (1) A transcription or arrangement should be viewed as a last resort; and under no conceivable circumstances should the *substance* of the music be altered; only its means of presentation. (2) Solo songs — and this refers to art songs and not to folksongs — should never be subjected to choral treatment. Had the composer felt that his composition was better suited to group expression than to a solo voice he would have written it for chorus.

[8] The taste and ingenuity of the arranger will often be tested in the writing of certain figures typical of strings, let us say, in terms of pianoforte style.

they are quite correct) or, having familiarized themselves with the harmonic background, they devote the left hand to its maintenance, inject what figuration is possible into the right hand part, and anchor the whole thing down with a sixteen foot pedal as convenience dictates. It is not beyond belief that if some enterprising musical missionary would undertake to make available even a few of the greater sacred works with the orchestral part adapted to organ style and planned with an eye to the capabilities of the not too average organist, the field of church music would be notably enriched.[9]

ORCHESTRAL ACCOMPANIMENTS

For choral compositions of larger dimension intended for concert performance, an orchestral accompaniment is generally provided. It goes without saying that the successful accomplishment of this task requires, first, a full command of orchestration. That the writing of accompaniments to vocal music does not demand a special type of orchestral knowledge is evidenced by the paucity of literature on this subject,[10] as well as by the inclusion of a surprisingly large number of accompanied choral works among the illustrations of methods of regular orchestral scoring. Berlioz,[11] for better or worse, pays a good deal of attention to the question of orchestral accompaniment, and offers not a few stimulating examples. But most text books either ignore the matter or, at most, touch on it lightly. What cannot fail to impress one in the orchestral illustrations drawn from choral works is the almost invariable superiority of the orchestration over the choral writing. In fact, if we disregard all questions of musical quality, it must be admitted that too

[9] In publishing organ accompaniments, no separate staff for the pedals is necessary. The use of the abbreviations "Ped." and "Man." and the downward projecting of the stems of those notes which are to be played by the feet will make the intention sufficiently clear.

[10] The reader is referred to Forsyth's *Choral Orchestration* (H. W. Gray and Co., 1920), for a consideration of certain fundamental matters relating specifically to the orchestral accompaniment of choral music.

[11] *Modern Instrumentation and Orchestration,* translated by Mary Cowden (London: Clarke-Novello, second edition, 1858), pp. 177-198.

many choral compositions prevail largely because of the orchestral gifts of their composers. This cannot be held to refer to Bach's monumental contributions to choral literature, for Bach, though far from skilled as a choral technician, was so great a musical architect that to him any form of disproportion was unthinkable. It does apply in great measure, however, to the works of Berlioz, and it certainly is pertinent to the choral compositions of Beethoven. Nothing but the genius of that composer makes the choral part of the finale to the *Ninth Symphony* tolerable. In order to lessen the vocal strain, the movement is sometimes transposed down one tone and when humane conductors cut the Gordian knot by omitting the voices entirely, the movement stands forth as one of the greatest of Beethoven's orchestral creations. Both Bach and Beethoven apparently thought of voices much as they thought of instruments, as more or less objective conveyances of musical ideas, and neither one — though this is truer of Beethoven than of Bach — ever conceded much to the limitations peculiar to vocalists. Certainly neither would be called a "singers' composer." [12]

It would not be true to say that exactly the reverse is applicable to Brahms, for orchestration was far more native to him than choral writing was to either Bach or Beethoven. Yet Brahms, in spite of the fact that he stands as a choral star of the first magnitude, was guilty of orchestral ineptitudes in his accompaniments. His treatment of the woodwind in particular is often irritating. Time and again the unearthly beauty of a choral passage is destroyed by the intrusion of the oboe; and more than one conductor's soul has been severely tried by the entrance of the woodwind in final cadences at a range which makes pianissimo playing difficult if not impossible. [13]

A rare and striking instance of equal power in both the choral

[12] Beethoven's vocal fugues are literally negative counsels for the choral composer. The lines seem to have no inner purpose and, in the case of the alto and tenor, often suggest badly written viola parts. See the fugues in the choral section of the *Ninth Symphony,* and "Et Vitam Venturi" in the *Missa Solemnis.*

[13] It may be questioned whether it is justifiable to do so, but the fact remains that some conductors strike out the woodwind parts in the closing sections of many of Brahms's choruses.

and orchestral fields is afforded by the composer Holst. In such works as *The Hymn of Jesus* and the *First Choral Symphony* there is an abundance of material for study in both orchestration and vocal writing. Furthermore, Holst, in spite of his amazing grasp of the resources of each, never exploits one at the expense of the other. There is an invariable and satisfying reciprocity which results in complete formal and artistic unity. The same may be said of Debussy and of Vaughan Williams whose *A Sea Symphony* and *Sancta Civitas* are to all intents and purposes textbooks on the art of orchestral and choral writing combined. It is the conductor more than any other who gratefully appreciates this power of adjustment between the two performing bodies; any accompanimental orchestra of full modern proportions which sets its entire roster including brass and percussion against the voices of the chorus is likely to create a problem in balance; yet there is, perhaps, no more satisfactory effect in music than the full orchestra, dynamically controlled and skilfully distributed, set as a background for vocal color. On the other hand, there are, indubitably, passages and whole movements where the style of the orchestral writing and its opulence seem to imply that what the composer wishes is that the sonorities of the orchestra shall be allowed full scope. At such points the choral writing is generally rhythmical and the text of a more or less incidental nature. Such accompaniments conform to the second division of type four.[14]

It is not the size of the orchestra but the scoring which counts. The young composer may profitably remember that the warrior is not less important than his weapon. Neither Samson nor David had at his disposal a division of field artillery; and Bach, in the "Cum Sancto Spiritu" of the *B minor Mass,* with an instrumentation of relatively modest dimensions, wrought an

---

[14] Cases of this kind are the exception and not the rule, and to admit their validity in no way contradicts the fundamental precept that practically all choral works take their sanction from a text which must be heard and understood. Where text repetition is employed, the sense, once gained, will permit a heavier use of the orchestra; and where repetition is oppressive an orchestral fortissimo may even be welcome.

accompanimental texture of such surpassing brilliance that it remains unchallenged in its field. Now if it is the conductor who is quickest to appreciate skill in the distribution of choral and orchestral resource, it is the composer who realizes to the full how disastrously calculation may fail when his work is confided to a director lacking insight and imagination. Not only is the conductor charged with interpretative matters; all the mechanics of performance, as well, are in his control. He is, furthermore, the mediator between the unexpressed intentions of the composer and the printed score. In any performance, vocal or orchestral, these responsibilities are not light, and when orchestra and chorus are combined the burden is a double one. This reference to the conductor in a work addressed to the composer is by no means irrelevant; for inasmuch as success or failure may conceivably hinge on those peculiarly complicated matters — particularly balance — which are an inevitable part of any joint choral and orchestral performance, the composer should resort to the written word in all cases where he fears that his wishes may be misinterpreted by the conductor. And, most emphatically, he would do well to under — rather than over — score his accompaniment.[15] If a work is of chamber character (which does not necessarily imply brevity) the orchestration should be of chamber dimensions; possibly strings, woodwinds, including horns, harp, and organ with light percussion. In any case, the numerical strength of the chorus cannot enter into the composer's calculation regarding the size of the orchestra. The modern chorus, unlike that of the eighteenth century, is frequently an imposing body, but no conductor who has at his disposal only a few singers is likely to attempt the performance of a work in which his chorus would be hopelessly overpowered even were the orchestra restrained to an unnatural degree. To say, as Berlioz did,[16] that an orchestra of one

[15] In connection with this matter of reticence in scoring, mention has already been made of the reduction of the choral parts to unison or octave writing. More than one textbook on orchestration calls attention to the fact that the reverse method is also advantageous; namely, writing for the chorus in parts, while the orchestra plays in unison.

[16] *Modern Instrumentation and Orchestration*, pp. 241, 242.

hundred and nineteen would require a chorus of one hundred and twenty-six is not tenable, because the volume of large choruses is sometimes no greater than that of smaller ones. Everything depends on the character of the voices and the training to which they have been subjected. Let it be repeated, then, that it is not the size of the orchestra which must concern the composer, but the *scoring*.[17]

Certainly one aspect of the composer's art will be displayed in the establishment of a safe margin of balance between the two performing bodies; a margin large enough to allow for differences of skill and perception in conductors, and for variations in the numerical make-up of different choruses. The scope, flexibility, and variety of the modern orchestra make this possible. These qualities, too, permit the composer not to think consistently in terms of general scoring, but in terms of the particular orchestral touch which supplements and heightens vocal color.[18] It is a question, of course, whether, in view of its all-embracing powers, composers have not tended gradually to commit to the orchestra too many of those devices which voices, by their nature, may justly claim as primarily their own, and which, because striking choral effects are comparatively few, the chorus can ill afford to sacrifice. One of these, certainly,

[17] For an amazingly astute use of limited choral and orchestral resources, see Hindemith, *Frau Musica,* which is written mainly for two vocal parts with accompaniment of strings and flute. Similarly Gluck's setting of the *De Profundis* for mixed chorus is characterized by restraint in every particular and is most appropriately scored for these few instruments: horn, alto, tenor and bass trombones, oboe, bassoon, viola, 'cello, double bass, and organ. Interesting examples of combined vocal and orchestral color are Stravinsky's *Les Noces,* the scoring of which includes mixed chorus, four pianofortes, tympani, xylophone, bell, tambourine, triangle, large and small cymbals, side drum, drum (without snare), and bass drum. Also *Flos Campi* by Vaughan Williams written for mixed chorus, flute, oboe, clarinet, bassoon, horn, trumpet, harp, celesta, triangle, cymbals, bass drum, tabor, and strings. The chorus vocalizes throughout in changing color. For this the directions include *ah, ur,* half-closed lips, close gradually, lips nearly closed, closed lips, extreme head voice.

[18] See the passage for high trumpet in Holst's *A Hymn of Jesus* on p. 24 (full score, p. 55), the bass drum and organ pedal on p. 17 (full score, p. 40) of the same work; the total scoring on p. 33 (full score, p. 57) to the end of Stravinsky's *Symphonie de Psaumes;* and as an example of text reinforcement, Brahms's employment of the bovine-sounding horns at the words "So be ye patient" on p. 17 (full score, p. 31) of the *Requiem.* Passages like these show to what advantage the imaginative composer may employ the modern orchestra.

is brilliant grouping. Brahms would not be deemed less sensitive to choral effect than Handel, yet it is evident that in climactic places Brahms displaced Handel's sonorous and tight-fisted chords with others which put much more dependence on orchestral volume. On the other hand, the greater flexibility and delicacy of the later orchestra has encouraged composers to exploit types of grouping, especially in the lower register, which the eighteenth century less frequently employed.[19]

It is generally agreed that the combining of men's voices with brass instruments is appropriate. The affinity between these two groups was established by nineteenth-century composers who imitated brass and especially horns in their choral writing. In the use of brass as an accompaniment for this medium percussive instruments offer a valuable reinforcement, and the maximum of effect is achieved (as with all instruments) by exploiting the brass as a choir independent of the voices.[20] Indeed, it should constantly be kept in mind that the orchestra admirably supplies two elements in which voices are deficient — variety of color and percussion; yet the chorus, within its limits, is capable of producing an individual and a stimulating color of its own. Hence, any long continued doubling of one voice by instruments, or of one group of voices by a group of instruments, often results in a loss of character on the part of each. For example, the composer who, at any point, desires the individual quality and sonority of the brass choir never adds the horns, because even at their brassiest horns lack the vitality of sheer brass tone; and in like manner the effectiveness of pure choral tone may be materially lessened by excessive instrumental doubling over a long period, especially when the orchestration

[19] At the end of the "Crucifixus" in Bach's *B minor Mass* will be found the low vocal grouping which was so widely used in the romantic period. But here Bach uses only the continuo with the voices. In Verdi's *Requiem*, however, similar low grouping will be found on pp. 178 and 179 with instrumental accompaniment.

[20] For an artful combining of men's voices, brass, and percussion, see Holst, *A Dirge For Two Veterans*, and Converse, *Laudate Dominum*. And for brilliant scoring of brass instruments and mixed voices, see the "Tuba Mirum" in Verdi's *Requiem*, the "Unfold Ye Portals" in Gounod's *Redemption*, and the "Tuba Mirum" in Berlioz' *Requiem*.

remains unchanged. Even should there be no brief *a cappella* passages — though these are eminently desirable — the most telling accompanimental scoring will be that which takes advantage, particularly by the use of solo instruments, of those orchestral factors which contrast with but are not hostile to vocal color.[21]

Most difficult of classification and most devastating of all instruments in its capacity for negativing both instrumental and vocal color and for reducing an entire score to the status of an amorphous tonal generality, is the organ. While it is desirable that the choral composer should have practical knowledge of the workings of the various instruments, familiarity with the mechanical adjuncts of the organ and with its style is especially necessary. The subtleties of organ technique as well as the inflexibility of organ structure render impractical and even impossible many passages which on paper appear effective.[22] On the whole, however, the offenses of the organist far exceed those of the composer, and for this reason it is of the utmost importance that the organ part should be written out in full. Dynamic indications should be plentiful; but registration, other than such general suggestions as "reeds with mixtures" or "8 ft. only" may be omitted because the stops on any two organs, even by the same maker, will certainly differ. The organ is, in a sense, the maid-of-all-work in the accompanimental score, and if its use is left to the discrimination of the organist, it may be absent when it is most needed, or, worse, it may be a constant and uniform undertone throughout the performance. In contrapuntal writing, above all, the use of the organ requires great judgment, as, being essentially a chordal voice in the orchestra, it may blur the melodic progress of the instruments especially in their lower range.

[21] No body of instruments either singly or in combination presents so many pitfalls in accompanimental writing as does the woodwind.

[22] One modern choral work in which the organ is employed requires the player at a certain point to use both hands and both feet and at the same time effect a crescendo. This, as any organist knows, is physically impossible unless a helper is at hand to draw the necessary stops.

In orchestral accompaniment, as in orchestration in general, strings are the foundation. It has been earlier mentioned in this book that there is a strong bond between strings and voices, and the exceptional range covered by the string choir as well as its dynamic and technical versatility allows the composer to take advantage of this natural relationship between the two groups. Even when doubled at the same range, or confined within the same compass, the mutual loss of tonal character seems to be less than in other cases. The danger is, of course, that the composer will neglect to avail himself of those powers which the string band possesses and which voices do not have, such as extensive range, great dynamic variety, muted effects, and pizzicato; and that he will too consistently rely on strings to fill out the body of his scoring because he knows that of all the departments of the orchestra they can be counted on to blend well with voices and to afford a discreet balance in all circumstances.

The importance of key selection in unaccompanied writing has earlier been dealt with, but as a factor in accompanied choral writing the choice of key is no less a matter of concern. We associate care in this regard with the routine of the orchestral or band composer. He knows the tonalities which are friendly to the technique and the sonority of a single family of instruments, and he realizes, further, that the quality of brilliance or restraint which pervades a whole movement will be controlled in no small degree by the given key. Such refinements hardly enter into the choral composer's calculations, because the human voice is subject to no such accurate predictions with regard to tone or technical ability as is an instrument. But in works where the orchestral part is viewed by the composer as significant — and few in the common repertoire fail to meet this requirement — purely instrumental considerations such as key selection should be given weight.[23]

[23] Mendelssohn must have been extremely sensitive to the relation of key selection to total effectiveness. One often wonders whether he did not, perhaps, change the key of some of his oratorio choruses after the movement had been completed, so

I cannot believe that any good end would be served by the submission of brief musical examples setting forth successful formulae for orchestration with chorus. Beyond a few broad observations as to the proved fundamentals of accompanimental orchestration and the mention of some isolated examples of effective procedure, it would not be profitable to go. If the student will first achieve competence in choral technique and orchestration, if he will study scores and listen critically to rehearsals and performances, he will be able to judge of the comparative value of the orchestral accompanimental practices of different composers and eventually establish a method of his own.

In concluding this matter I cannot do better than to point to the example of Berlioz who acquired his basic knowledge of orchestration by inducing instrumentalists to try out for him experimental passages (and in this I doubt not he often made a nuisance of himself), and by observing during performance the effects resulting from transference of the symbols of the score into sound. A thorough practical knowledge of instrumentation gained by these or any other means, together with an understanding of the technique of choral writing, should be the musician's possession if he expects to write competently a choral work involving the participation of both singers and orchestra.

---

unerring was his faculty for making the crucial sections monuments of choral and orchestral rightness.

CHAPTER VI

SPECIAL CHOIRS

CHORAL COMPOSERS have, for the greater part, cultivated the medium of the mixed chorus in preference to isolated subdivisions like men's voices and women's voices, and this is not remarkable when one considers the limitations inherent even in music for a chorus which includes both sexes. Literally to cut in halves the restricted resources of range and color which, at the most, a mixed chorus may command, is to invite a compensating quality of excellence in the music itself that has seldom been realized. Any roster of composers of music for men's or women's voices separately is notable chiefly for the absence of great names. Furthermore the output of those really distinguished men who have written for these special choirs is comparatively small and consists mainly of brief compositions. It would be natural to suppose that singers would elect that music which is most interesting because of its variety even if they could not be counted on to choose what is aesthetically superior. The fact remains, however, that choruses of men's voices and of women's voices are comparatively numerous; a phenomenon which explains itself as soon as one realizes that the spirit which animates most of these organizations is not musical but social, or is dictated by necessity as in men's or women's colleges, where one or the other group must be used exclusively. The demand for music on the part of these groups is large, and the supply is ample, even if it is not uniformly admirable.

A work of the dimensions of a cantata in which the choral sections are exclusively for men's or women's voices should avail itself of the most varied orchestration in the accompaniment; it should include solo voices, especially sopranos and altos if the main body of the composition is for the lower voices, and tenor and bass if a women's chorus predominates.[1]

Unless from the urge of economic necessity the young composer is not advised to devote himself intensively to composition in these artistically rather unrewarding fields. But inasmuch as he will doubtless have occasion in the course of any choral work to write short passages or, in a longer work, a whole movement, for a single section of the chorus, he ought to be acquainted with the main principles which underlie composition for these special choirs.

MEN'S VOICES

Even a moderately large experience of men's voices will reveal three facts: first, that no vocal group possesses such a capacity for richness as do tenors and basses; second, that a chorus so constituted is incorrigibly monochrome; and third, that no other choral medium is, by nature, so completely independent of accompanimental support. While the first is unquestionably a virtue, that virtue may be, and often is, converted into a defect when richness is overemphasized by the injudicious use of chromatics. The pervading fullness which characterizes the tone of a men's chorus needs to be occasionally reduced if it is not to be oppressive; but if that richness is enhanced by the sentimental chromatic devices to which it seems so easily to fall a prey, the effect may then become inexpressibly cloying. Any chord bearing more than one chromatic alteration should be viewed by the composer with suspicion, unless the chromatics contribute something of a dissonant nature, or are inevitable in the voice leading. The chromaticism

[1] With what varying degrees of success composers have been able to inject interest into an extended work for men's voices may be gained by a study of the scores of the following works: David, *The Desert;* Bruch, *Frithiof;* Goetz, *The Waterlily;* Mendelssohn, *Festgesang;* Cherubini, *Mass in D minor;* Brahms, *Rhapsodie;* Stravinsky, *Renard* and *Oedipus Rex.* For women's voices: d'Indy, *Saint Mary Magdalene;* Smart, *King René's Daughter;* Pergolesi, *Stabat Mater;* Vaughan Williams, *Magnificat;* Bendall, *The Lady of Shalott;* Caplet, *Le Miroir de Jésus;* Debussy, *The Blessed Damozel;* Chabrier, *The Shulamite.*

represented in Example 149 illustrates the excessive use of this feature. Not only is the texture of the music overlush, but such persistent use of color accidentals is bound to lead to tonal uncertainty.

EVENING SONG · 3,4.

Ex.149.

Reger.

stars ——— a - shine that our God hath kin - dled.

O, the still - ness, O, the still - ness, O, the still - ness!

The reduction in fullness just mentioned is achieved by the use of unison (octave) and two- or three-part writing. This may be done in one of two ways: either a whole work or an occasional passage may be written in one, two, or three parts, or individual chords may be so treated.[2] A splendid example of clarity without loss of body is the following specimen of three part writing (Ex. 150). Groupings like the following are useful (Ex. 151). Where doubling takes place the balance between the parts should be preserved. Thus if three voices are united on one pitch the fourth will probably be sadly overtopped, especially if one of the doubled notes lies in its upper range. Example 152 shows how effectively customary four-part harmony may be relieved by other groupings. Figures indicate the number of separate pitches in each chord.

Another reason for the frequent breaking down of the traditional four-part arrangement is found in the fact that sooner or later the music will descend to a range at which four-part writing, if consistently employed, will result in thickness and possibly in gruffness. Chords similar to those in Example 153

[2] In this case four-part harmony may be taken to indicate chords in which each of the four voices sings a different pitch even though there be but three factors in the chord.

had best be avoided except for special effect, and the dynamic indicated should never be louder than piano.

Men's voices produce such a wealth of overtones that any crowding of even three parts into a lower register is bound to produce a fuzziness and obscurity in the sound. Indeed, the third of the chord may sometimes be omitted with salutary results. When it is present, however, it needs to be placed high enough to allow the chord to speak freely. Example 154 presents a most effective negation of this generally valid principle. Here the composer wishes to give the effect of a hushed murmuring, and therefore groups the factors of the chord, including the third, in a deep register. This, however, represents a very special effect.

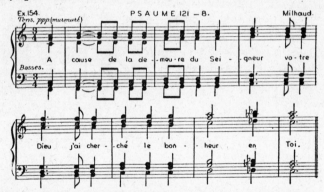

Chords of the seventh, ninth, eleventh, and thirteenth are of great assistance in counteracting by dissonance the prevailing tendency toward over-richness, but the greatest care should be exercised lest they defeat the purpose they serve so well. In other words, the factors of these chords must be selected with an ear to sonority and color. The question is not of including as many notes as possible, but of employing the right ones, which, incidentally, will be to a not inconsiderable extent those which do not involve the singers in difficulties of intonation. The following types of grouping will be found rewarding (Ex. 155).

Ex. 155.

Inverted positions of these chords are highly desirable but the problem of factor selection is, in their case, even more acute. Groupings like these are entirely practical (Ex. 156). The spacing of such chords should generally be open and the approach to the dissonant members should be secure, preferably by suspension, or by one of the methods mentioned on pages 42, 43.

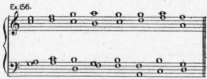

Ex. 156.

The inescapable uniformity of the tone color of a men's chorus makes imperative the employment of every resource of variety. Each voice should, as far as possible, traverse a wide range, and the grouping should frequently be altered to take advantage of the contrast between close and open spacing. The total range is, at best, small, and too often composers fail to utilize notes which lie above *A* or *B* flat in the first tenor because of prejudice against the falsetto voice. Chest quality, however, cannot be maintained indefinitely in its upper register, and unless head tones are used, the composer neglects to avail himself of a means that well serves the purposes of color contrast, and which is, when appropriately and skilfully used, of a rare and ethereal beauty.[3] In this book the author at least

[3] Head tones are not the exclusive property of tenors, but head-tone color is, to be sure, most effective in the upper voices.

once advises the use of the written word as a means of making clear the effect the composer wishes to attain, and in this case, again, it would seem to be desirable to do so. Many chorus tenors object to using the falsetto voice as they consider it a trifle unmanly. But even more, they are persuaded that fading off in the upper register will be taken as a sign that they are not real tenors at all.[4] Hence, if the composer, for reasons which may be valid, wishes at any point a light, misty quality, he had best do more than indicate it by the customary dynamic marks. He should write over the music "head tone" or "falsetto"; otherwise he may be rewarded with that peculiarly vibrant, gritty tone which is an almost invariable feature of typical pianissimo "Männerchor" singing in the upper register. A further distraction from the prevailing monotony of men's voices may be offered by the use, in accompaniment, of the upper register of the pianoforte or of instruments like the flute, harp, celesta, and violin in a comparatively high register.

But the most rewarding avenue of interest, especially under conditions of limited range, and in *a cappella* style, is opened up by the employment of rhythmic variety. One has but to imagine the unhappy result of the transposition of Examples 157 and 158 into a homorhythmic order.

The tonal self-sufficiency of the men's chorus and its close-knit texture make unaccompanied writing for this medium its most telling conveyance; and this is true especially in the shorter forms in cases where text and style suggest such a treatment. But there occur short compositions which for obvious reasons require some instrumental commentary. Then the accompaniment may assume a good deal of independence; indeed, it may approach the proportions of a separate instrumental piece.[5] For reasons which have been touched on in the pre-

---

[4] Without intending to be ungracious, it must be said that this kind of unreasonable supersensitiveness is more characteristic of the choralist than of his orchestral brother; the author has never known one instrumentalist who felt that he was sacrificing his artistic dignity by playing harmonics.

[5] For a splendid example of skill in supplying a characterizing orchestral part, at the same time permitting the men's voices to stand out independently, see Franck, "Chorus of Camel Drivers" from *Rebecca*.

ceding paragraphs, a large proportion of pieces for men's voices are comparatively brief. But of all the natural limitations which circumscribe the technical and artistic scope of this type of writing, none is more drastic than the enforced absence of counterpoint.[6] It will be noted that thus far in this chapter technical procedure has been dealt with in terms of harmony. Part-writing in the field of men's voices is, to a great extent, a matter of chord-to-chord progress. The crossing of the parts is

[6] It would interest the student to observe how often passages which begin bravely in fugal style conform rapidly to the inevitable devices of harmony.

more or less of a gesture because of the similarity in color between any two adjacent voices; and anything like a far-flung
melodic line (unless it is an outer voice) is bound eventually
to lose itself in the mass and merge in one uniform color. Thus
the manipulation of the substance found in Examples 155 and
156 is not really difficult because the composer may plan the
introduction of dissonant factors within a comparatively small
area of the music. Without the presence of counterpoint any
choral music is at a very great disadvantage, and where the
difficulty of sustaining interest is multiplied, as it is in this
medium, every substitute for real counterpoint should be
invoked: separate entrances, however brief; frequent rests in
each part; and above all, a rhythmic variety distributed among
the various voices.[7]

Women's Voices

Practically all the physical and artistic circumscriptions which
beset composition for men's voices, with still others, must be
overcome by one who would write successfully for a chorus of
women. Here is a medium which unlike men's voices is not
rich in sound, and is more markedly monochrome. Counterpoint, furthermore, is of even less use, because women's voices
are more similar in character than men's and their range is
less wide. Hence, all the available substitutes for counterpoint
recommended in connection with men's voice writing are
doubly desirable here. These are artistic considerations, and
they do, to be sure, weigh heavily enough. But the most persistent enemy against which a chorus of women's voices must
war is the fact that it is fundamentally and inescapably a super-
structure. Twenty minutes of unaccompanied singing in this
medium will lead most hearers, I believe, to yearn ardently for

[7] In those works for men's voices written by either Mendelssohn or Brahms the
student will find excellent examples of sound method. See also: Borodin, *Serenade;*
Poulenc, *Chanson à Boire;* Bax, *Now is the Time of Christymas* and *The Boar's Head;*
Elgar, *After Many a Dusty Mile;* Schmitt, *De Profundis;* Sibelius, *The Broken
Melody;* Holst, *Choral Hymns from the Rig Veda* (4th group) and *Before Sleep;*
Ropartz, *Embarque;* and Pizzetti, *Per un Morto.*

the presence of a bass. This sense of incompleteness has generally been compensated for in various ways; chiefly by limiting *a cappella* compositions in this field to pieces of comparative brevity, by the use of instrumental accompaniment, and by frankly replacing chords in fundamental position by inversions.

In reference to the first, it may be said that though modern composers have endeavored to offset the innate deficiencies of the women's chorus by applying color in the form of successions of closely spaced chords and by the revival of mediaeval devices based on organum they have only succeeded in fending off for a little longer the inevitable saturation point to which prolonged singing in this medium is bound to lead. The formulae included in Examples 159 and 160 are effective, but they represent pure color and frank archaism, and neither of these will stand long exploitation.

The addition of an accompaniment is advisable in any piece for women's voices which extends beyond three or four octavo pages in length. By this means almost all the resources of much needed variety may be introduced and, at the same time, a true and satisfactory bass may be supplied. Although in every type of choral accompaniment a single note in the bass may well be reinforced at the octave, in the instrumental part of a composition for women's voices it is doubly desirable. Another advantage arising from the use of an accompaniment is that it leaves the second alto free to remain a melodic rather than a

harmonic voice. Second basses supply an admirable foundation,
but second altos, partly because of their quality, which is not,
save in exceptional cases, markedly different from that of the
first altos or even of the second sopranos in their lower range,
and partly because of their small compass, are rarely successful
in assuming the functions of the "dominant-tonic" bass. *A
cappella* writing for women's voices in which the second alto
is assigned the rôle of a true bass must be cast in a key which
allows the second alto to descend to the tonic and sing it with
enough volume to make it impressive; and unless the upper
voices are crowded down within a small compass, this limits
the choice to five, or at the most six, tonalities. Composers have
naturally been unwilling to submit to such a restriction, and
in cases where the alto could not effectively reach the fundamental, they have generally, in the absence of an accompaniment, substituted a first inversion for the normal root-position
chord. Familiarity with *a cappella* singing by women's voices
has accustomed us to accepting this compromise and it has
come to be a tradition in such music. It is a none too happy
solution, however, and an accompaniment makes it unnecessary. Example 161 is a splendid case of the belated completion
of the 6/4 chord by a root in the accompaniment. The effect
here is so beautiful that we cannot believe it to be a compromise.
Nonetheless, the fact remains that *E* flat is not within the compass of the alto voice.

Two- and especially three-part writing for unaccompanied
women's voices is satisfactory, and while the employment of
four parts is practical, it is generally most effective when an

accompaniment is present. As in the case of men's voices, chords of the seventh, ninth, eleventh, and thirteenth are very useful, and if the tenor and bass of the chords in Example 155 are moved up an octave they will serve equally well for women's voices. A compact arrangement of the notes of a seventh or higher powered chord results in striking sonorities and colors (Ex. 162 *).[8] As in the case of men's voices, the more dissonant

THE SHEPHERDS OF THE DELECTABLE MOUNTAINS-29.

effects must be carefully introduced according to methods already suggested. In a single instance, however, preparation is not necessary, namely in a succession, usually diatonic, of identically constructed chords (Ex. 163). Writing in thirds and sixths is invariably helpful, perhaps because of the basically harmonic character of music for women's voices, and the device of the "sweep" in the form of a triad repeated in different positions, or diatonically, is so germane to the character of the

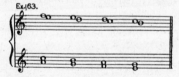

medium that composers have used it over and over again. Two instances are given (Exs. 164 and 165).[9]

[8] For another felicitous application of this principle see Holst, "Funeral Chant," *Hymns from the Rig Veda,* Group 2, No. 3.

[9] For varying solutions of the challenge offered the composer by the limitations

The author realizes that he has made out a by no means ingratiating case for these special choirs of men's and women's voices, and he is perhaps too conscious of their defects as individual organizations because of a long and concentrated association with them which has persuaded him that their chief utility consists in furnishing contrast the one to the other.

Preoccupation with mediums which are, at best, representatives of a truncated artistic life appears as an anachronism in an age which recognizes as never before the mutual contributions of the sexes to every form of artistic enterprise. One could not seriously plead for the abolition of men's and women's choruses, but most musicians, we may believe, would heartily welcome a closer union of Cecilia with Apollo.

---

of women's voices, see the following: Holst, *Choral Hymns from the Rig Veda* (Groups 2 and 3); Mendelssohn, *Drei Motetten;* Wagner, "Chorus of Flower Maidens" (*Parsifal*); Brahms, *I Hear a Harp* and *Song from Ossian's Fingal;* Stravinsky, "Unterschale" (*Vier Russische Bauernlieder*); Schubert, *23rd Psalm.* See also *Selected List of Choruses for Women's Voices* (Smith College Monographs, No. 2) by Arthur W. Locke which supplies a large quantity of material in this medium and which will shortly appear in a revised edition.

CHAPTER VII

THE TEXT

IN CHOOSING a text the composer should give especial heed to three considerations. He should seek words embodying ideas which stimulate his imagination; he should, save in very exceptional cases, confine himself to material of a high literary quality;[1] and he should be sure that the text he selects literally cries out to be sung. That is, he should be sure that it is not only lyrical in the poetic sense, but that, as a matter of practical workmanship, it will also *sing* admirably. Indeed, the distinction between lyrical poetry and singers' poetry is no imaginary one.[2]

Regarding the admonition that the composer should employ only texts of high literary quality, it may be said at once that the history of music offers much by way of rebuttal. Although many composers have been unable to arouse themselves to creative effort in the face of an inferior text, others, and great ones, have been quite impervious to this consideration: Monteverdi whose madrigals are often little more than strings of lachrymose expletives, Schubert whose literary sense where poetry was concerned was frequently deficient, Rameau who certainly lives by his music and not by the librettos he set, Bach who poured out the noblest musical commentary on words that were far from meriting his consideration, and Handel spread-

[1] A translation is generally less desirable than its original, unless the original is cast in a language unfamiliar to the average chorus. Translations are even less artistically valid than musical transcriptions for they do not even sound like their originals, and much poetry, though fitted out with calculated devices like alliteration and onomatopeia, depends to a not inconsiderable extent for its effect on the mere sound of the words.

[2] This matter is not the least subtle among those which the choral composer is called upon to face. He will find many valuable suggestions in H. C. Colles, *Voice and Verse* (London: Oxford University Press, 1928), and in J. P. Dabney, *The Musical Basis of Verse* (New York: Longmans, Green and Co., 1901).

ing his endless roulades over verbal inconsequentialities and capping the whole by a resounding musical phrase on the words, "Whatever is is right." Indeed, when one reviews the extraordinarily beautiful music which composers have been able to supply for sheer literary nonsense, we marvel that the Elizabethans with the transcendent poetry at their disposal did not rise to even greater heights if such a thing were possible. If only for his own self-respect as an artist the conscientious composer will not willingly be wanting in literary discrimination, nor will he wish to risk the reservations of the singers or the public concerning his sense in this matter. On the other side there are certain texts which, like some folksongs, appear to fulfil so completely their own destiny that any attempt to heighten their significance borders on the impertinent. One is constantly asking himself, "Why has no composer ever added music to these words?" But second thought will often reveal the reason, for either because of a literary virtue so rare that it even suggests silent rather than audible reading, or because of association with deeply poignant moments in human experience, these words reject the accompaniment of music however eloquent. In the same way one may ask what painter could hope to match on canvass the imaginative power of the verbally sparse account of Elisha beleaguered in the city of Dothan at the moment when the eyes of the terrified servant were opened and he saw the mountain "full of horses and chariots of fire." [3]

If, however, some composers draw back before a degree of imaginativeness that defeats musical intention, others delight in setting texts of a distinctly prosaic and even factual nature. One wonders whether literature of this kind is not as self-sufficient, as unfriendly to musical accompaniment as the other. Not a little earthy writing belongs in the field of modern poetry, and as poetry one need have no quarrel with it. The question is solely as to whether music at its best — and no other degree of excellence is worth consideration — belongs with poetry of this nature.

[3] II Kings, ch. 6.

> Fat black bucks in a wine-barrel room
> Barrel-house kings, with feet unstable,
> Sagged and reeled and pounded on the table,
> Pounded on the table,
> Beat an empty barrel with the handle of a broom,
> Hard as they were able,
> Boom, boom, BOOM,
> With a silk umbrella and the handle of a broom,
> Boomlay, boomlay, boomlay, BOOM.[4]

This verse can be set to music and it has been, but it would seem that any addition of music must result only in an unwarranted though slight distraction from the ideas expressed in the poem. Both language and music are self-sufficient, having rights of their own, and when these rights conjointly minister to the ends of beauty, music and language will combine effectively, but when either music or language becomes predominant, the other loses its effectiveness and becomes decadent.

For substantially the same reason it is difficult to feel any enthusiasm for settings of humorous texts. Among these are not included pieces of a light or sportive nature such as the "Scherzo" from Holst's *First Choral Symphony* composed to words by Keats, but rather those whose frank purpose is to cause laughter. In instrumental music the same distinction may be drawn. The "Scherzo" from Mendelssohn's Opus 20 whether played by strings or in its orchestrated version may, if you wish, be interpreted as the spirit of humor in music; and it is quite different from a piece which provokes mirth merely by tricks of orchestration or the employment of bizarre musical ideas. The capriciousness of Mendelssohn's music might make you smile, but it would not make you laugh. The humor that abides in music is by nature different from that conveyed in words. Therefore there can be no partnership on an equal basis. Humor stands alone in this regard. Happiness, serenity, sadness, exuberance, fantasy, these, when expressed in language, may find appropriate conveyance through music. In choral literature, music maintains two important rôles: of making evocative not

[4] Vachel Lindsay, *The Congo and Other Poems* (New York: Macmillan, 1914); quoted by permission of the publisher.

the words but what lies hidden within them, and of *suggesting* rather than *describing*. In most humorous choral music, at least, the words are one-dimensional, proceeding in a straight line without any implications of a deeper meaning, involving the hearer in little more than is presented by the *sound* of the words; and the music, if not actually descriptive, closely approaches that function.

Those considerations which affect the singing quality of a text might be made the subject of an entire volume. The all-important test of fitness, however, is performance. After making his selection, the composer should literally live with the words, singing them over and over and improvising the music. Then he will observe what is awkward from the vocalist's standpoint, and if there are not too many of these instances, and their clumsiness is not irremediable, he may devise ways of circumventing them. Little by little his perception of the beauty of the text will deepen, and with this will grow an ordering and a stabilizing of musical ideas.

Vowels and consonants make up the substance of words; vowels are the flesh, consonants the bones. They are interdependent, yet each possesses its own function. Clearly, it is the consonants that are the more influential for good or ill. Vowels are so adaptable by reason of the many ways in which they may be vocally treated that they need not be a serious concern. No wise composer, however, will ask a chorus to sing on a high note *ee* as in seek, *e* as in left, *i* as in lift, *o* as in low, *a* as in wade, or *u* as in full or mute. The guiding principle of so setting a text that the most is made of its lyrical possibilities is *distribution,* not only in a single part but in all the voices as they sound together, and the reigning principle in that distribution is a naturalness that lies as close as possible to speech. This applies not only to syllables and whole words, but also to vowels and especially to consonants taken by themselves. For example, *s, ss, t, q,* and even other consonants rapidly repeated throughout the parts may make a normally singable passage sound painfully disturbing. And even more difficult are those cases in which consonants either singly or in combination tend to absorb the vowel sound, becoming, themselves, the vocal agent. Under such circumstances only a pinched and arid delivery can ensue.[5] It would take a skilful choral composer to convert the following passages into terms of vocality.

> See where she sits upon the grassie greene,
>   (O seemely sight!)
>   *A Ditty* — Edmund Spenser [6]

> She's somewhere in the sunlight strong,
>   Her tears are in the falling rain,
> She calls me in the wind's soft song,
>   And with the flowers she comes again.
>   *Song* — Richard Le Gallienne [7]

> When the pods went pop on the broom, green broom,
>   And apples began to be golden skinn'd,
> We harbour'd a stag in the Priory coomb,
>   And we feathered his trail up-wind, up-wind.
>   *A Runnable Stag* — John Davidson [8]

The element in any text most desired by the singer is spaciousness, and this means simply a preponderance of "uninhibited" vowels. Lines like these are more or less ideal as a framework for vocal music:

> Fair and fair, and twice so fair,
>   As fair as any may be;
> The fairest shepherd on our green,
>   A love for any lady.
>   *Fair and Fair* — George Peele [9]

> And sometimes thro' the mirror blue
> The knights come riding two and two:
> She hath no loyal knight and true,
>   The Lady of Shalott.
>   *The Lady of Shalott* — Lord Tennyson [10]

---

[5] When there is a deliberate effort to convey disagreeable ideas by means of verbal cacophony the composer should not, of course, attempt to destroy the author's intention.

[6] *Oxford Book of English Verse, 1250–1918* (London: Oxford University Press, 1940), p. 111.

[7] *Oxford Book of English Verse*, p. 1080.

[8] *Oxford Book of English Verse*, p. 1040.

[9] *Oxford Book of English Verse*, p. 150.

[10] *Oxford Book of English Verse*, p. 841.

One of the keenest disappointments the choral composer can experience is the realization that his neatly planned staccato passages have failed in effectiveness. Let the student try to sing with irreproachable crispness the following phrase from Sullivan's *Echoes:*

> When, rous'd by lute or horn, she wakes
> And, far away o'er lawns and lakes,
> Goes answering light!

The composer has given the tempo as "allegretto" and has written "staccato" over the vocal parts at this and other points. The music is homophonic and the effect is obviously intended to resemble the orchestral pizzicato. Only a chorus of exceptional technical skill, however, could hope even to approach the ideal of a true staccato. Here it is the distribution of the consonants which, in the main, causes the difficulty. Every syllable and every word should be clearly separated from its neighbor, but this is almost impossible of achievement when *n* is followed by *r* ("when roused"), *d* by *b* ("roused by"), and *d* by *f* ("and far"). "By lute," moreover, will almost certainly emerge as "Bylute," "lawns and lakes" as "lawnsun lakes," and "far away o'er" as "farawayo'er." In general, words which end in *s,* and conjunct words, the first of which ends and the second of which begins with a vowel, are poor material for staccato singing. In these and other cases the composer who asks for a staccato is asking of the singers something which is against nature, and the conductor, after a few efforts to realize the composer's intentions will generally be content with a gasping delivery of the words that is exhausting for the singers and painful for the audience. The ideal of a not too-rapid staccato as precise as the pizzicato is not unattainable, but the composer must choose his text with care and he will do well to suggest in a footnote the method (if he knows by experience that it will succeed) by which a choral staccato is to be obtained.

Vowels are the composer's golden opportunity. It is through these that he enunciates the gospel of vocality. By spreading a single vowel over several measures, for example, the singer is given time to express the full meaning of the text at that point, and to impart to the music all the beauty of sound of which he is capable.[11] Naturally, this principle of vocal expansiveness is not universally applicable, and when exaggerated it leads to artificiality, but even this is preferable to overcrowding a choral score with text. This method, so disastrous to good vocal effect, represents, I doubt not, the revolt of certain composers against the preciosity inherent in over-vocalization. Quite rightly they desire that their text arrangement shall follow as nearly as possible the principle of normal utterance. But they forget that the singing of words which one would ordinarily speak is in itself artificial; that in choral music verbal activity is generally four times multiplied; and that the process is transformed into art only by the application to it of such good taste and insight as will endow it with the convincing semblance of reality. A superfluity of text generally leads to two faults. The large number of words sung causes the music to sound choppy and restless, and, in extreme cases, reduces the chorus to mere chattering.[12]

Another disadvantage of a crowded text is that it often makes necessary a persistent repetition of words and phrases. Plainsong almost never repeats either its text or its music for purely artistic reasons. The repetition of either text or music merely for the sake of spinning out the musical substance to greater lengths is indicative of a secondary interest in the words. Folksong, in contrast to plainsong, repeats the same music in spite of changing text situations and sometimes merely strings "fa la's" or proper names together as an excuse for providing just one more hearing for a lovely tune. This is a frank and reasonable use of repetition, and I think we may assume some text repetition generally necessary in vocal composition, but where words continue to be exploited merely to furnish occasion for continued musical effort, the practice is certainly open to

[11] See the Examples on pp. 56 and 57.

[12] For a deliberate and extremely clever use of overtexting see Janequin, *Le Caquet des Femmes;* and for a generally unhappy result due to word-congesting see *On Himalay* by Bantock.

scrutiny. Gluck, in the preface to *Alceste,* was very clear on this question of text repetition, and although his pronouncement had beneficial results, too few composers, alas, have given heed to his words.

The complete abandonment of text originates in the composer's desire for color effect, for contrast, or to be rid of the distraction of verbally expressed ideas and the percussive interruptions of consonants. Textless vocal music is an unquestioned resource, especially when used as accompaniment, but it must be employed with nice discrimination and above all, reticently. What makes vocal music individual is that, unlike instrumental music, it is accompanied by words, and it is those words from which the music springs.[13] Presumably the text conveys a continuously developed idea, and to interrupt it by humming or *oo*-ing and *ah*-ing for any but a sound reason is generally questionable practice. All efforts, and there have been conscientious and skilful ones, to sustain interest throughout an extended *a cappella* vocal work written without words have failed. Quite aside from any question of the logical application of the device, the monochrome quality of voices and the absence of those multiple features that make orchestral music stimulating defeat any attempt to use vocalizing *in extenso.*

The temptation to run after vocal opulence gained by such means as have just been described sometimes leads the composer to forget one prime requisite of all choral music, namely, that the sense or meaning of the words shall always be clear. On the other hand, if persistently treated in harmonic style where verbal coincidence is uniform throughout the voices, the words may lose something of their imaginative power.[14] This apparent

[13] D. B. Munro, in *The Modes of Greek Music* (Oxford: The Clarendon Press, 1894), p. 120, points out that the Greeks admired vocal music because a text embodied ideas which music could make articulate — a function denied to instrumental music. And he cites the following passage from the Aristotelian *Problems* which declares that "the human voice (too), is comparatively without charm if it does not represent something."

[14] Most of us are familiar with the church that was designed to be especially effective for preaching, and where because of a lack of any reasonable resonance the speaker's meaning is evident almost before the words which convey it are spoken. When language conduces to thought, there is both emotional and intellectual profit

contradiction embodies a subtle and sorely neglected issue, and the ineffectiveness of not a little choral music is due to the failure of composers to deal with it intelligently. There is a desirable mean between text treatment that results in obscurity and one that yields over-clarity. In real counterpoint, where the words almost never fall together, the skilful workman will so distribute the crucial sections of the text that the meaning of the whole is clear. Admittedly this is a problem involving careful calculation, and one that may be mastered only, perhaps, after long study and experience.

Every choral composer should aim to set his words with "just note and accent," as Milton phrased it, and among the many French composers who have been noteworthy apostles of this gospel none was more conscientious than Lully. It is evident from his instrumental works that Lully possessed at least a respectable melodic sense, but in his recitative-like arias he concentrated relentlessly on declamatory truth. A greater musician than Lully, however, was the Englishman Henry Purcell, a composer who was not only faithful to his text, but one who could also write superb music to accompany it. When William Byrd spoke of vocal music that was "framed to the life of the words" he was unconsciously prophesying the work of Purcell. "Framed to the life of the words" is an exact characterization of Purcell's music. Not only does that music illuminate every shade of meaning, but the subtlety with which the words are underlaid often sets the modern singer a task, for unless he is careful he will find himself distributing the syllables in a manner different from that indicated by the composer. While a skill like Lully's or Purcell's is a sure sign of the expert craftsman, the student should not view mastery of text distribution as no more than a tool of his trade, for it must be a vital part of his ambition to make his music at every point the complement of the ideas set forth in the text. The union will be for him complete and unbreakable.

---

in being a trifle ahead imaginatively, and a bit behind mentally. Indeed, an infinitesimal time-lag is the friend of eloquence whether in speech or in music.

In attempting to bring about an identity of purpose between text and music the composer has at his disposal three main approaches. The first and most obvious is through word-painting; the naïve imitation by the music of what might be called the exteriors of the text. The French chanson composers of the early sixteenth century employed it to a wearisome degree, and many a later writer has not scorned to use it. One may doubt, however, whether many would now feel that they had struck very deep if they did no more than make a melody go up at the words "He ascended into heaven," or write a diatonically descending phrase to characterize a less happy experience. A really superb use of pictorial writing, however, is to be found at the end of the chorus "O Thou that tellest good Tidings to Zion" in the *Messiah,* where at the word "rising" Handel achieves much more than routine description. Second and certainly more subtle is the expression in the music of what the text *suggests;* to characterize, rather than to paint; to hint, in diverse musical ways at what lies just below the surface of the meaning.[15] Purcell, again, was a past master of vocal characterization. In the funeral anthem "Thou knowest, Lord, the secrets of our Hearts," the words "But spare us Lord most holy; O God, most mighty" are set to music predominantly minor. The word "mighty," however, is accompanied by a resounding major triad that seems to suggest not so much the idea of might, as it does that salvation is an assured consequence of prayer to divine omnipotence. The passage which closes the chorus "All We Like Sheep Have Gone Astray" from the *Messiah* demonstrates perfectly how music may suggest the idea resident in the words. When Handel approached the phrase "But the Lord hath laid

[15] The various musical methods of interpreting the meaning of words, as well as all other ramifications of the relationship between text and music, have throughout the ages furnished musical theorists and writers on aesthetics with material for debate. In no other department, save, perhaps, that of the ethical content of music, have opinions ranged so widely from the naïve to the profound. *Musica reservata* of the sixteenth century was concerned with the matter of making the meaning of the words articulate in the music, and later generations gave much attention to the word *affekt,* which stood, in part at least, for the means by which various emotions might be expressed in music.

on Him the iniquity of us all" he showed himself the great man he was by abandoning the tepid musical formulae of the period — formulae which constitute the body of the chorus — and by writing music which magnificently mirrors the scriptural text at every point. Particularly at the long-held last inversion of the dominant seventh chord which accompanies the word "Him" does one feel the magnitude of the iniquity.[16]

But the third and most telling resource is the magic formula which has ever been the property of the few; the "rubbing together" of words and music until they appear to possess a common significance. When every shade of meaning in a text is reflected with the utmost fidelity, when the musical setting is so knit together with the verbal substance that, even though the words be withdrawn, their spirit and their literary personality seem still to pervade each note of the choral texture, then, indeed, you discover what skill and insight can achieve when combined to fuse text and music into one entity. It is no new accomplishment, this integrating of words and music, for some of its most artful manifestations are to be found in the works of late fifteenth- and early sixteenth-century composers. If, for example, you take only the music of the following passage from Josquin's *Ave Christe* (Ex. 166) you are amazed at its immo-

Ex. 166.   AVE CHRISTE IMMOLATE - 43.

Des Près.

- rum, Sa - lus et | spes in - fir mo - | rum,   Sa -

lus et spes in - | fir - mo - | rum,   Sa-

[16] In the same way that Haydn's strutting and self-important aria in *The Creation*, "In Native Worth and Honor Clad," is a delightful though perhaps unintentional parody on the vanity of mankind, so Handel, in the *Messiah*, used the text "And great was the company of the Preachers" as a vehicle for one of the most repetitious and boresome choruses on record.

bility. Surely Josquin, with his prodigious technical mastery, could have avoided such long emphasis on a single musical figure; indeed, it is not until you read the words "spes infirmorum" — "hope of the ailing" — that you come upon the secret, for to those words Josquin has written the most depressing, bed-ridden music imaginable. Here a single thread of feeling runs through both members of one body; it has been called the "inner nerve of the text" and fully to express it in music is no uncertain mark of genius.

CHAPTER VIII

FORM

THE WORD "form" as applied to choral music has two meanings. The first refers to type, the second to structure. Choral types are, for example, the madrigal, chanson, frottola, oratorio, cantata, and part-song. Also to be included under this head are sacred works like the motet, Mass, and anthem whose titles are associated specifically with the church. To these may be added such types as carols, passions, and requiems, the nature of whose texts is revealed by their names. Among works which may be identified by their conformity to a technical or structural pattern are the round, the catch, and the fugue. Some choral pieces are obviously subject to both classifications; to a generic and to a structural one. Thus multitudes of folksongs (generic) are cast in binary, ternary, or rondo form (structural).

Almost from the beginning many of the generic titles assigned to choral music have been to some extent ambiguous. Choral composers of the sixteenth century delighted in multiplying generic designations, but it sometimes happens that the contemporary prescriptions as to what a certain type should embrace are not fulfilled by the music itself. At a later period confusion is not lessened by the fact that in some cases vocal and instrumental music employ the same generic titles; the words "air," "song," and "rhapsody," for instance, are used interchangeably. And finally, the caprice of modern editors in selecting titles to describe certain items in their catalogues which are, assuredly, far from their earlier counterparts, and the indifference of composers to fundamental distinctions between various classes of choral music such as accompanied and unaccompanied have rendered generic differentiations almost meaningless. A further

bar to the establishment of clean-cut distinctions between forms
exists in the fact that any new form begins by adopting something from a previous period, continues by developing its own
characteristics, and finally remains fixed at its full stature or becomes merged with a succeeding form as was true of the Italian
madrigal. In any event, the age-long confusion that has resulted
from attempts to classify choral forms accurately, especially
where more or less similar types were concerned, has resolved
itself in our time into a general distribution of all choral music
into one of six fields: sacred, secular, accompanied, unaccompanied, long, and short. The oratorio and the sacred cantata,
though their differences were doubtless once clear, are generally
specified as one or the other on the basis of length. Even so,
disagreement will inevitably arise with regard to the first two
classifications, sacred and secular. An uncritical world now sees
no difference between the music of the madrigal and the Mass,
with the result that the text is left as the only determining
factor.

Briefly then, formal titles for choral pieces may be said to
have little significance in our day. Length may have some bearing on the question, but the only decisive ascription possible is
provided by the nature of the words. All choral works with text,
regardless of their music, are either sacred or secular. Beyond
that point it is impossible to go with certainty where generic
titles are concerned.

The foregoing refers mainly to what a piece of choral music
is called. Those structural elements it contains and which accord
it continuity and integration are another matter. In the fifteenth
and sixteenth centuries composers could not, of course, draw on
instrumental music for architectural models. The reverse was,
in fact, the case. Bald repetition such as Handel frequently employed at the beginning of his choruses, and the somewhat more
subtle sequence, a constant in eighteenth-century music, were
not common in the church music of the Golden Age, owing,
perhaps, to the fact that plainsong was not friendly to such
devices as drew attention to themselves. Yet the motets of the

period are marvels of unity. This is understandable when a plainsong cantus served as the animating and coördinating spirit throughout. But in many instances the problem is met in more ingenious ways; sometimes by almost regularly recurring passages in familiar and contrapuntal style, and again by the persistent use of a single interval. Indeed, these motets display admirably the basic formal principle of repetition relieved by contrast, a principle which appears in the first primitive music which uses repetition as an aid to memory, and, tiring of that repetition, introduces the brief contrasting phrase. The idea of repetition crystalizes in the use of the sequence, is extended to include imitation, and culminates in the fugue. In the choral fugue contrast is gained by the employment of alternating men's and women's voices, by changes of rhythm, by opposed passages in harmony and counterpoint, and by the multiple additional devices which make this form in the hands of an imaginative and skilful composer a stimulating and even an exciting piece of music. In the sacred choral music of the late fifteenth and the sixteenth centuries there is to be found a practice more significant for the student of choral forms than the purely technical devices just mentioned, and that is the adoption, for obvious reasons, of familiar style for the setting of passages of text which are of an especially devout character, or which are, so to speak, doctrinal key phrases. "Tu pauperum refugium," "ave Christe," "quia per sanctam crucem tuam redemisti mundum," and similar phrases are often treated in this way. Thus in these comparatively early pieces one discovers the clue to the whole philosophy of form as it applies to choral music, namely, that the form of any choral piece must, in the last analysis, depend on how the composer coördinates the musical ideas which spring from the shifting material of the text. Every change of thought, every dramatic moment, must find its complement in the music. Because of textual exigencies the music taken by itself may appear to be no more than a succession of unrelated passages. But when presented together with the text which inspired it, and knit together with such purely musical devices as

the ingenious composer may find appropriate, it may appear to
be as logical and integrated as though cast in sonata form. The
difficulty of imparting coherence to a brief musical work involving frequent changes of mood is considerably less when
an accompaniment is used. The instrumental prelude, the post-
lude, and the interludes, if similar in character, will furnish
unity to a degree usually not attainable in an unaccompanied
piece of like nature. The dilemma does not exist, of course, in
the forms listed at the beginning of this chapter as belonging in
a definite structural category — forms like the catch, the round,
and the fugue.

The fugue whose excellencies have already been suggested is
the most imposing of choral forms. From the composer's point
of view it possesses still another virtue in that it permits him to
escape for the moment from the persistent tyranny exercised
over him by the text. What the recitative was to the older opera,
the fugue is, in a sense, to a choral work of dimensions. The
recitative quickly disposes of batches of literary material necessary to the narrative but not, perhaps, particularly suitable as
the vehicle of ingratiating melody. The fugue invites vocal expansion; for the moment the composer may disregard many
conventions of text treatment; without pretending to make
sense he will repeat the same group of words without mercy.
If the recitative relegates music for the moment to the background, the fugue, in its turn, makes of the text a secondary
consideration. Both, again, afford variety and relief. The recitative mitigates the persistence of tunefulness, the fugue supplies
one close-knit element among a prevailing diversity of formal
types. One difficulty with the fugue, and one to which Bach was
occasionally indifferent, is the planning of the vocal entrances
so that they lie within the range of the voices to which they are
assigned. This means that modulations must be laid out in such
a way that the entrances are adequately separated by episodic
material and that the various tonalities selected for the entrances
will readily accommodate the range of the subject in all the
voices.

Another difficulty is that the first phrase of text is often the most salient one, and, as such, it is naturally used with the subject; from which it follows that in ninety-nine cases out of one hundred the subject will be sung to the same words. "And with his stripes we are healed," "The Lord led us on, for Him we contended" — such fragments bear an implication of continuity and we do not resent the composer's harping upon them. But when we hear the words "Our children's children shall rehearse thy deeds in never-dying verse" repeated over and over again we begin to have an acute distaste for heroic conduct. Anything like sensitive discrimination in this matter has been comparatively rare in choral music, for the truth is that the use of imitation or of the sequence spells intellectual preoccupation with musical matters, wherein the text and its meaning become of secondary importance. Perhaps the best proof of this is to try to find some text which immediately suggests to you imitation as its normal musical conveyance.

All in all, the writing of a good choral fugue is a task for the master craftsman, but at its best it is without a peer among choral forms.[1]

Not alone in the fugue, but also in those cases where some primarily instrumental form is superimposed upon the material, does the composer's responsibility toward the text become lighter. If this is in the nature of compensation, it must be said

---

[1] A study of the following fugues is suggested: Bach, "Through Thee, Our Guiding Light Supernal" (*Ode of Mourning*), "Lord, When our Haughty Foes" (*Christmas Oratorio*), "Gratias Agimus" (*B minor Mass*); Handel, "Then Shall They Know" (*Samson*), "They Loathed to Drink of the River" (*Israel in Egypt*), and the fugues in the *Messiah*, especially the "Amen"; Haydn, "Ach, Erhör unser Flehen" (*Tobias' Heimkehr*), "Direct us in Thy Ways" (*The Seasons*); Astorga, "Eia Mater" (*Stabat Mater*); Mozart, "Kyrie" (*Requiem Mass*); Graun, "Seine Tage sind abgekürzet" (*Der Tod Jesu*); Gounod, "Hosanna in Excelsis" (*Mors et Vita*); Rossini, "In sempiterna saecula amen" (*Stabat Mater*); Brahms, "But the Righteous Souls" and "Worthy Art Thou" (*Requiem*), "From Thine Abode" (*Make Me, O Lord God, Pure in Heart*); Schmitt, "Parceque le Seigneur est très élevé" (*Psalm 46*); Hindemith, "Es beugt die Häupter all" (*Das Unaufhörliche*); Stravinsky, "Expectans Expectavi Dominum" (*Symphonie de Psaumes*).

In particular, however, the student is referred to the opening chorus of Bach's cantata *Es ist nicht gesundes an meinem Leibe* (No. 25) which both in content and structural variety is a fugue to end all fugues.

on the other side that arbitrarily to employ instrumental forms in choral music too often leads to an artificial result. When this is not so, the composer's organizing power is invariably of a high order. To say that the heart of Bach's musical thinking was instrumental is to make no new observation. Singers are certainly well aware of its truth. It was natural, then, for Bach to look in many cases to instrumental forms for the outlines of his choruses.[2]

The cantatas are particularly rich in instances of this practice and the method employed is closely related to one or another of those which Bach cultivated for the organ and for the orchestra. So great is the affinity between the vocal and instrumental elaborations of the chorale that either one might have suggested the other. Granted that many of the chorale prelude choruses, particularly those in the later cantatas, are monumental works of art, one often feels, nevertheless, that preoccupation with architectural matters sometimes results in the absence of certain artistic values which are not lacking elsewhere in any of Bach's music; that had the musical ideas paid less tribute to formal demands and devoted themselves exclusively to an eloquent rendition of the text, the result would have been more spontaneous and a closer parallel to so many of his other choruses in which the interest is steadily cumulative.[3]

Handel's approach to the formal problem was not the one to which Bach so naturally turned. Handel could be routine, repetitious, and even downright dull, but when he was any of these

---

[2] An unusually successful application of one of the strictest and most limiting of instrumental forms, the *passacaglia*, appears in the "Crucifixus" in the *B minor Mass*. Bach employs it also in the final chorus of the cantata *Nach dir, Herr, verlanget mich* (No. 150).

[3] Choruses of the chorale prelude type in which there is close reference to the parent melody are mainly of two kinds: those in which the chorale is treated contrapuntally and those in which the different phrases are made the subjects of fugal passages. Examples of the former will be found in the cantatas *In allen meinen Taten* (No. 97), *Allein zu dir Herr Jesu Christ* (No. 33), *Was Gott tut, das ist wohlgetan* (No. 98), and particularly *Wachet auf, ruft uns die Stimme* (No. 140). The second type occurs in *Aus tiefer Not schrei' ich zu dir* (No. 38), *Nimm von uns, Herr, du treuer Gott* (No. 101), and notably in *Ein' feste Burg ist unser Gott* (No. 80).

the responsibility lay not with his constructive or imaginative power, but with the text itself. In most of his choruses a single idea or sentiment seems to run through the words, but where a change of meaning or feeling takes place he usually meets it frankly by introducing new musical material. Nor was he likely, in a lengthy chorus, to risk exhausting interest by exploiting a single musical idea for too long a period. In such cases, even when the general sense of the words remained unchanged throughout, he insured variety by calling in fresh musical reinforcements.

Choral music was considerably influenced by the formal definiteness so characteristic of the classical period. Both Haydn and Mozart reveal this fact in their music. In their choral style there is ample acknowledgement of Handel's genius, and Mozart often adopted Handel's formal procedure. Haydn, on the other hand, generally adheres to the classical idea of form. Compare, for example "When His loud voice in thunder spoke" from *Jephtha* with "The Heavens are telling" from *The Creation*. The length of both these pieces implies a structural problem. First, it is to be noted that both composers are dealing with texts of a somewhat similar character containing three separate phrases involving no violent change in sentiment, each of which is subjected to varying degrees of repetition. Handel takes one section of text, works it out and turns to the next, clothing it with new music. The three phrases of the Haydn, on the other hand, are all thematically related. Handel's key scheme represents a nice balance between tonic and dominant, but there is no reference at the end to the *material* of the first section. Haydn up to the last few pages departs from his original key only transitorily and after each excursion into new material returns to his primary statement with almost rondo-like insistence. After the opening dramatic section in homophonic style, Handel employs fugal treatment for the second and third parts and the developments are characteristic of Thorough-bass period *choral* music. But Haydn here rejects the fugal type for one that is, to be sure, contrapuntal and imitative, and which expands into a long-breathed development in classical *instrumental* style. The text is appropriately set in both cases, but it exerts little if any influence on the formal aspect of the music. Therefore, one may compare these pieces as abstract studies in choral form, and from that point of view the Haydn, though its text is shorter and its music longer than those of the Handel chorus, is much the more closely-knit of the two.

Haydn's chorus is in one sense a prophecy of the choral adoption of tri-partite form on a large scale, for it contains real development, but the realization of that prophecy has not been invariably happy. The application of the tri-partite principle to choral music demands unusual skill and insight. If anything like a sympathetic relationship between form and substance is to be achieved, two conditions must usually be present. These conditions are, first, that the final phrases of the text shall coincide with the initial ones,[4] and, second, that all the language shall be of such uniform import that a literal repetition of the music will do no violence to the sense of the words. In the first case, however, care must be taken that the intermediate phrases have not supplied a new significance to the final words even though they are literal repetitions, nor must the composer fall into the classic error of the Neapolitan *da capo* arias which merely reverted at the end to a statement whose dramatic force had already been expended.

It was Mendelssohn, as one might expect, who more than once adopted sonata form for his choruses. Thus, in "He watching over Israel" from *Elijah,* a first theme is announced in *D* major, followed by a second theme in the relative minor. There is development, recapitulation, and a brief coda. Essentially the same formal plan appears in his chorus for women's voices, "Laudate Pueri," the first of the *Drei Motetten.* Brahms's formal viewpoint was broader — perhaps he could not look at a text so dispassionately as could Mendelssohn. To be sure, the elements of instrumental form are sometimes to be found in Brahms's

[4] This condition is often met in folksongs and simpler choral forms in which a single mood prevails throughout. See, for example, Jannequin's *A ce joli mois.*

choral writing, particularly the rhetorical codas in the manner of William Byrd, but for quasi-sonata form he substituted repetition as the text allowed it, seeking to impose formal unity on a whole work rather than on a single movement, and to achieve integration by closely relating his musical ideas rather than by limiting them numerically and tonally in accordance with instrumental tradition. This must not be taken to mean that Brahms neglected the formal element in his shorter pieces or in the separate movements of the larger works. In fact, to the student of choral composition the resourcefulness, variety, and above all the subtlety exhibited by Brahms in creating a sense of unity under all conditions is not less amazing than his superlative way with the voices themselves.

Brahms's *Requiem*, in its separate choruses as well as in its totality, is a rewarding study of form as an element in choral music. If a passage of text is repeated, then repetition is clearly needed for emphasis or as a means of providing unity — never unity in the structural sense, but always because the mood of the movement demands it. Where the text of a single number is relatively long and the meanings so diverse as to forbid repetition, Brahms will close the movement with a fugue which both textually and musically appears as the dominating feature for which all the previous sections of material have been preparing. Nos. 3 and 6 are, from this point of view, triumphs of architectural skill. How sensitive he was to the importance of total unity and how skilful in turning the text to this end may be seen in the fact that the music which concludes the first and last choruses of the *Requiem* is the same, although the two passages of text have but one word in common. That word is "blessed," and its value as a pivot word referring both to "they that mourn" and to "the dead which die in the Lord" did not escape the composer. When a single movement presented no formal complications, Brahms often enough employed the ABA principle sometimes with modifications, or he invoked melodic and rhythmic reminiscences and suggestions which served to hold together different but related passages of text.

The *Schicksalslied* is a witness to the care Brahms took to observe the requirements of formal completeness in his choral works. Here the text offers a knotty problem. At the beginning it speaks of the peace and well being of the departed and at the end it draws a bleak picture of human despair. But Brahms apparently wanted to emphasize the beatific side of the text, and a less fastidious composer would simply have resorted to ABA form with a literal repetition of the text and music of the first section. Such a procedure would have been far too obvious and too artistically unsound in view of the diametrically opposed sentiments involved, and Brahms's solution was at once ingenious and perceptive. His orchestral prelude is relatively long, and it is faithful to the mood of the opening words. After the black mood of the close, then, he introduces again his opening instrumental commentary, which, being without words, recalls the serenity and elevation of the initial movement in a way which the presence of a text, with its clear-cut meaning, could not possibly do.[5]

Primarily, the question of form in choral music is not one belonging to a single period. From this point of view it may be said that modern composers have not made drastic departures from accepted method. However, the proverbial brevity of modern music often forbids the possibility of extended formal treatment, so that the ends of coherence are occasionally gained by the repetition of a single motif. In more extended movements an inevitably recurring idiom such as Holst's diatonic ostinato will often suffice. In one case, at least, Stravinsky employs elaborate academic machinery of a formal nature; this occurs in the second number of the *Symphonie de Psaumes* in which he announces a considerable fugue in the orchestra, then superimposes on the first fugue another to be sung by the chorus.

The foregoing brief references to different methods of bringing about formal coherence in choral composition are intended mainly as a suggestion for further study of this aspect of the

[5] Further examples of Brahms's structural versatility are the *Gesang der Parzen*, *Mary and the Boatman*, and *Der Gang zum Liebchen*.

subject, and as emphasis on the importance of the text as dictator of the formal scheme. One thing may be said with certainty. Even though the composer be lavishly equipped with all the devices necessary to make his choral music convincing as far as the effect of the voices, whether accompanied or unaccompanied, is concerned, he cannot hope for success unless he acquires the art of investing his work — however severe the task imposed upon him by the text — with logical continuity and with formal order.

APPENDIX

APPENDIX

GROUP I

NOEL · 28,29.   Saint-Saëns.

are the na·tions rag — — — ing?

ODE OF MOURNING · 5.   Bach.

flow-ing, the bit·ter tears — are flow·ing,

LE ROI MALGRÉ LUI · 150.   Chabrier.

Ah! —

THE MESSIAH · 81   Handel.

that tak·eth a·way — the sins — of — the world —

GROUP II

9TH SYMPHONY - 36..   Beethoven.

GROUP III

SCHICKSALSLIED - 6.   Brahms.

A SEA SYMPHONY -124.   Vaughan Williams.

GROUP IV

REQUIEM IN C MINOR -45.   Cherubini.

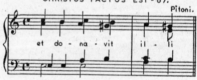

CHRISTUS FACTUS EST - 67.   Pitoni.

KING ARTHUR - 21.   Purcell

GROUP V

Copyright in U.S.A. and all countries, 1929, by the Oxford University Press, London.

GROUP VI

MASS IN B FLAT MAJOR - 22.

THE MESSIAH - 124.

GROUP VII

DER GANG ZUM LIEBCHEN - 5.

VESPERAE DE DOMINICA - 21.

TE DEUM - 115.

DIFFUSA EST GRATIA - 80.   G.M. Nanino.

in la - bi - is, in la - - - - - bi - is tu - - - is,

GROUP VIII

THE BEATITUDES - 42.   Franck.

Swift by life's tem-pest we're dri - ven,

Trem - bling our hearts shrink with fear;   Storm - toss'd

THE SEASONS - 86.   Haydn.

a - way, a - way, ah, let - - - us. fly.

REQUIEM IN C MINOR - 16.   Cherubini.

cum re - sur-get cre-a - tu-ra, cum re - sur-get cre-a - tu-ra,

GROUP IX

1ˢᵀ CHORAL SYMPHONY - 92.   Holst.

THE PRINCESS ULALIA - 12,13.   Malipiero.

ALLELUIA - 12.   Randall Thompson.

GROUP X

STABAT MATER - 81,82.

Dvořák

THE RIO GRANDE - 6,7.

Lambert.

Group X, *continued*

REQUIEM - 4,5,6.   Delius.

GROUP XI

GROUP XII

GROUP XIII

ST. PAUL -176.

Mendelssohn.

stone him to death, stone him to death!

TOBIAS' HEIMKEHR-62.

Haydn.

wahr - haft, hei - - lig, al - - les um - fas - send,

THE BEATITUDES-63.

Franck.

Her ter - ri - ble fea -tures haunt ev' ry dream.

GROUP XIV

MORS ET VITA - 36.

Gounod

co-qet om - nes an -te Thronum, co-qet om - nes an - te Thro- - -

THE HARP THAT ONCE THRO' TARA'S HALLS-3,4.

Hindemith.

now - - - - - hangs as mute on Ta - ra's walls as

if that soul - - - - - were fled. - - - - - So

THE BEATITUDES -118.   Franck.

King all glo--rious! Rise vic-to-rious! Might-y God!

GROUP XV

THE BIRTH OF VENUS -9.   Fauré.

sighs,.... The air o'er-fill---ing.... With words of love,

PARADISE LOST -102.   Dubois.

Flames that for ev-er bound us, Fearful that rise a-round us,

GROUP XVI

L'ALLEGRO -97.   Handel.

thee, Mirth, with thee we mean to live.

MASS IN C MAJOR - 43.   Haydn.

re - sur-rec-ti - o - nem,

GROUP XVII

GROUP XVIII

THE CREATION - 49. Haydn.

DAS UNAUFHÖRLICHE - 4,5. Hindemith.

GROUP XIX

THE RIO GRANDE - 8. Lambert.

ORPHEUS - 47,48. Gluck

GROUP XX

GROUP XXI

GROUP XXII

REQUIEM MASS - 12.

Mozart.

Sol - vet saeclum in fa - vil - la. Tes - - te Da - vid cum Si - byl - la,

MANFRED - 30.

Schumann.

Sops.

He ga - zeth, He ga - zeth, From his glance the sun - beams flee;

Altos.

Tenors.

Basses.

He moveth

GOD'S TIME IS THE BEST - 4.

Bach.

be - ing, as long, - - - - - as long as He wills.

GROUP XXIII

THE CREATION - 37.

Haydn.

state - - - - - - ly dress,

1ST CHORAL SYMPHONY - 36.

Holst.

bliss, For ev - - er wilt thou love, and she be fair!

LORELEY - 22.

Mendelssohn.

And the storm thro' the wild wel - kin dash - - - - - - - -

GROUP XXIV

SONG OF PRAISE - 6,7

LASSET UNS ABLEGEN DIE WERKE DER FINSTERNIS - 13,14.

GROUP XXV

GROUP XXVI

REQUIEM MASS - 26.

Pizzetti.

GROUP XXVII

STABAT MATER -13,14.

GROUP XXVIII

KING DAVID -82.   Honegger.

When waves of death en-com-passed me, And snares of men made me a-fraid, Then did he send, and take me from a-bove, And drew me forth out of ma-ny wa-ters.

SCHICKSALSLIED -14.   Brahms.

-en, Like spray of the cat-a-ract

LIST OF PUBLISHERS

ABBREVIATION	PUBLISHER
A	Augener Ltd., London
AMP	Associated Music Publishers, Inc., New York
AS	The Arthur P. Schmidt Co., Boston
B	Boosey & Hawkes, Inc., New York
BB	Ed. Bote & G. Bock, Berlin
BH	Breitkopf & Härtel, Leipzig
BM	The Boston Music Co., Boston
C	J. Curwen & Sons, London
CCB	C. C. Birchard & Co., Boston
CEMI	Casa Editrice Musicale Italiana, Florence
D	Durand & Cie., Paris
E	Enoch & Cie., Paris
ECS	E. C. Schirmer Music Co., Boston
ER	Édition Russe de Musique, Paris
F	Foetisch Frères, Lausanne
FH	The Frederick Harris Music Co. Ltd., Oakville, Ontario
GS	G. Schirmer, Inc., New York
H	J. Hamelle, Paris
Has	Carl Haslinger, Vienna
HD	H. F. W. Deane & Sons, London
He	Ad. Henn, Geneva
Heu	Heugel & Cie., Paris
HWG	The H. W. Gray Co., Inc., New York
JF	J. Fischer & Bro., New York
JWC	J. & W. Chester Ltd., London
Ka	Kallmeyer, Wolfenbüttel
L	Laudy & Co., London
Lit	Litollf, Braunschweig
M	A. Z. Mathot, Paris
MM	Murdoch, Murdoch & Co., London
N	Novello & Co. Ltd., London
OD	Oliver Ditson Co., Philadelphia
OUP	Oxford University Press, London
P	C. F. Peters, Leipzig
R	G. Ricordi e C., Milan
RL	Rouart, Lerolle et Cie., Paris

ABBREVIATION	PUBLISHER
S	N. Simrock, Berlin
SB	Stainer & Bell, Ltd., London
SC	Schola Cantorum, Paris
Sch	B. Schott's Söhne, Mainz
TJ	Tischer & Jagenberg, Cologne
U	Universal-Edition, Vienna

INDEXES

INDEX OF COLLECTIONS

Collections containing a piece of music to which specific reference is made, or from which an excerpt is drawn, are supplied with abbreviations. (PL indicates engraver's plate number.)

ABBR.	TITLE	PUBLISHER	DATE OR OTHER IDENTIFICATION	PAGE
DC	Chorwerk, Das (ed. Blume)	Wolfenbüttel: Kallmeyer	1929–1938	104 *n*
	Denkmäler der Tonkunst in Bayern	Leipzig: Breitkopf & Härtel	1894–1937	104 *n*
	Denkmäler der Tonkunst in Österreich	Vienna: Artaria	1894–1937	104 *n*
	Denkmäler Deutscher Tonkunst	Leipzig: Breitkopf & Härtel	1892–1937	104 *n*
DV	Deutsche Volkslieder, 2 vols. (Brahms, arr.)	Leipzig: C. F. Peters	(I) PL 10201 (II) PL 10202	35 *n*
EMS	English Madrigal School, The (ed. Fellowes)	London: Stainer & Bell Ltd.	1913–1924	104 *n*
HC	Hindemith-Chorlieder für Knaben	Mainz: B. Schott's Söhne	1930	104 *n*
	Hispaniae Schola Musica Sacra (ed. Pedrell)	Barcelona: Pujol	1894–1898	104 *n*
HRV	Choral Hymns from the Rig Veda			
	Group 1	New York: H. W. Gray Co., Inc.	1911	104 *n*
	Group 2	London: Stainer & Bell Ltd.	1912	139 *n*
	Group 3	London: Stainer & Bell Ltd.	1912	139 *n*
	Group 4	London: Stainer & Bell Ltd.	1912	135 *n*
IeM	Instituzioni e Monumenti de l'Arte Musicale Italiana	Milan: G. Ricordi e C.	1931–1934	104 *n*
LAM	L'Arte Musicale in Italia	Milan: G. Ricordi e C.	1897–	104 *n*
	Laudate Pueri (ed. Tovey)	London: Augener Ltd.	1910	64 *n*

ABBR.	TITLE	PUBLISHER	DATE OR OTHER IDENTIFICATION	PAGE
LdM	Livre des Motets, Ire Année (ed. Bordes)	Paris: Schola Cantorum	PL S1G–S40G	
MM	Monteverdi, Madrigale (ed. A. Mendelssohn)	Leipzig: C. F. Peters	No. 3232C	
	Monteverdi, Tutte le Opere (ed. Malipiero)	Asolo	1926–1932	104 n
MSP	Musica Divina (ed. Proske)	Regensburg: Pustet	1853–1855	104 n
NOA	Musica Sacra (ed. Commer)	Berlin: Ed. Bote & G. Bock	1839–1887	104 n
NOC	Musica Sacra, vol. I (ed. Dörffel)	Leipzig: C. F. Peters	PL 7215	104 n
NPB	Novello's Octavo Anthems	London: Novello & Co. Ltd.	——	
	Novello's Octavo Choruses	London: Novello & Co. Ltd.	——	
	Novello's Part-Song Book	London: Novello & Co. Ltd.	——	
	Sammlung Vorzüglicher Gesangstücke (ed. Rochlitz)	Mainz: B. Schott's Söhne	1838–1840	104 n
SRP	Schütz, Sämmtliche Werke (ed. Spitta)	Leipzig: Breitkopf & Härtel	1885–1894	
	Songs of the Russian People (Schlindler, arr.)	Philadelphia: Oliver Ditson Co.	1915	
WB	Tudor Church Music	London: Oxford University Press	1923–1929	104 n
	William Byrd, Collected Vocal Works (ed. Fellowes)	London: Stainer & Bell Ltd.	1937–1939	
WerB	Works of Henry Purcell, The	London: Novello & Co. Ltd.	1878–1928	104 n
	L. van Beethoven's Werke	Leipzig: Breitkopf & Härtel	PL 207 B	

INDEX OF COMPOSERS AND COMPOSITIONS

Pages indicated in italics contain a musical excerpt. Those in roman contain only a reference to a composer or a composition. (PL indicates engraver's plate number.)

COMPOSER	COMPOSITION	VOLUME	PUBLISHER	DATE OR OTHER IDENTIFICATION	PAGE
	Non vos Relinquam	WB VII			31 n
	Praise our Lord all ye Gentiles	EMS XVI			26, 31 n
	Sacerdotes Domini	WB V			31 n
Caplet	Inscriptions Champêtres		D	1918	136
	Miroir de Jésus, Le		D	1924	91, 128 n, 139
	Trois Chants d'Église		D	1920	136
Carissimi	Kyrie	LAM V			104 n
Carter	Defense of Corinth (MS)				90
Carver	O Bone Jesu		HD	1926	96 n
Chabrier	Roi Malgré Lui, Le				95 n
	Shulamite, The		E	PL 1348	88, 112, 165
Cherubini	Requiem in C minor		BM	1917	128 n
	Requiem in D minor		P	PL 8985	21, 82, 110, 166, 169, 173
			P	PL 6175	115 n, 128 n
Chopin					3
Converse	Laudate Dominum		GS	1906	123 n
Cui	Two Roses, The		GS	1898	19
David	Desert, The		N		128 n
Debussy	Blessed Damozel, The		GS	1903	120
	Pelléas et Mélisande		D	1907	128 n
					64 n
	Trois Chansons		D	1908-10	18, 30, 31 n
					5, 6
Delius	Requiem		U	1921	87, 104 n, 172

COMPOSER	COMPOSITION	VOLUME	PUBLISHER	DATE OR OTHER IDENTIFICATION	PAGE
	First Choral Symphony		N	1925	66, 89, 120, 142, 170, 179
	Funeral Chant	HRV II No. 3			138*n*
	Funeral Hymn	HRV I No. 3			18
	Hymn of Jesus, The		SB	1919	63, 75, 91, 105*n*, 120, 122*n*
	I Love My Love		C	1917	35*n*, 54
	Matthew, Mark, Luke and John		C	1917	35*n*
	Swansea Town		C	1917	33*n*, 35*n*
	There Was a Tree		C	1917	35*n*
Honegger	King David		F	1925	23, 25, 27, 91, 109*n*, 186
Humphrey	—		H	PLJ 2438 H	99*n*
d'Indy	Chant de la Cloche, Le		D	1895	19, 87, 98*n*
	Fervaal		RL	1924	90
	L'Histoire du jeune Soldat		RL	1924	35*n*
	Lisette		RL	1924	35*n*
	Querelle d'Amour, La		BM	1905	128*n*
	St. Mary Magdalene	IEM VI			95*n*
Ingegneri	Dolorosi Martir		U	1928	24, 83
Janáček	Festliche Messe		L	PLJ 770L	159*n*
Jannequin	A ce joli Mois		RL	1924	146*n*
	Caquet des Femmes, Le				98
Kastalsky	—				

COMPOSER	COMPOSITION	VOLUME	PUBLISHER	DATE OR OTHER IDENTIFICATION	PAGE
Pitoni	Christus Factus Est	LdM	R		63, 166
Pizzetti	Per Un Morto		R	1926	135 *n*
	Requiem Mass		R	1923	104 *n*, 183
	Rondine, La		R	1926	98 *n*
Poulenc	Chanson à Boire		RL	1923	90, 135 *n*
Praetorius	———	——	——		5
Purcell	King Arthur	——	——		148
	O Sing unto the Lord	NOA	N	PL 8259	166
	Thou Knowest, Lord, the Secrets of Our Hearts				22
Rameau	———	——	ECS	1925	149
Ravel	———	——	——		140
	Trois Chansons				8
Reger	Evening Song		D	1916	24
Rimsky-Korsakoff	———	——	BM	1911	129
	Spinning Top, The				8
Ropartz	Embarque!		OD	1915	35 *n*
Rossini	Messe Solennelle		D	1926	135 *n*
	Stabat Mater		OD	1869	29, 167
Roussel	Padmâvatî		N		41, 57, 156 *n*
	Psalm 80		D	1919	77, 134
Saint-Saëns	Noel		CCB	1929	47
	Nuit, La		OD	1877	165
			D	1900	137